In honor of

Mary DeLoney

for supporting the
CALS Foundation
2015

AT HOME IN **Sri lanka**

AT HOME IN Sri Lanka

PHOTOGRAPHS BY JAMES FENNELL

TEXT BY TOM SYKES

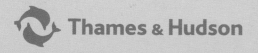
Thames & Hudson

First published in 2016 in hardcover in the United States of America by Thames & Hudson Inc., 500 Fifth Avenue, New York, New York 10110

thamesandhudsonusa.com

Library of Congress Catalog Card Number 2015953615

ISBN 978-0-500-51840-3

Printed and bound in China by Shanghai Offset Printing Products Ltd

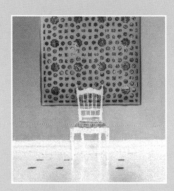

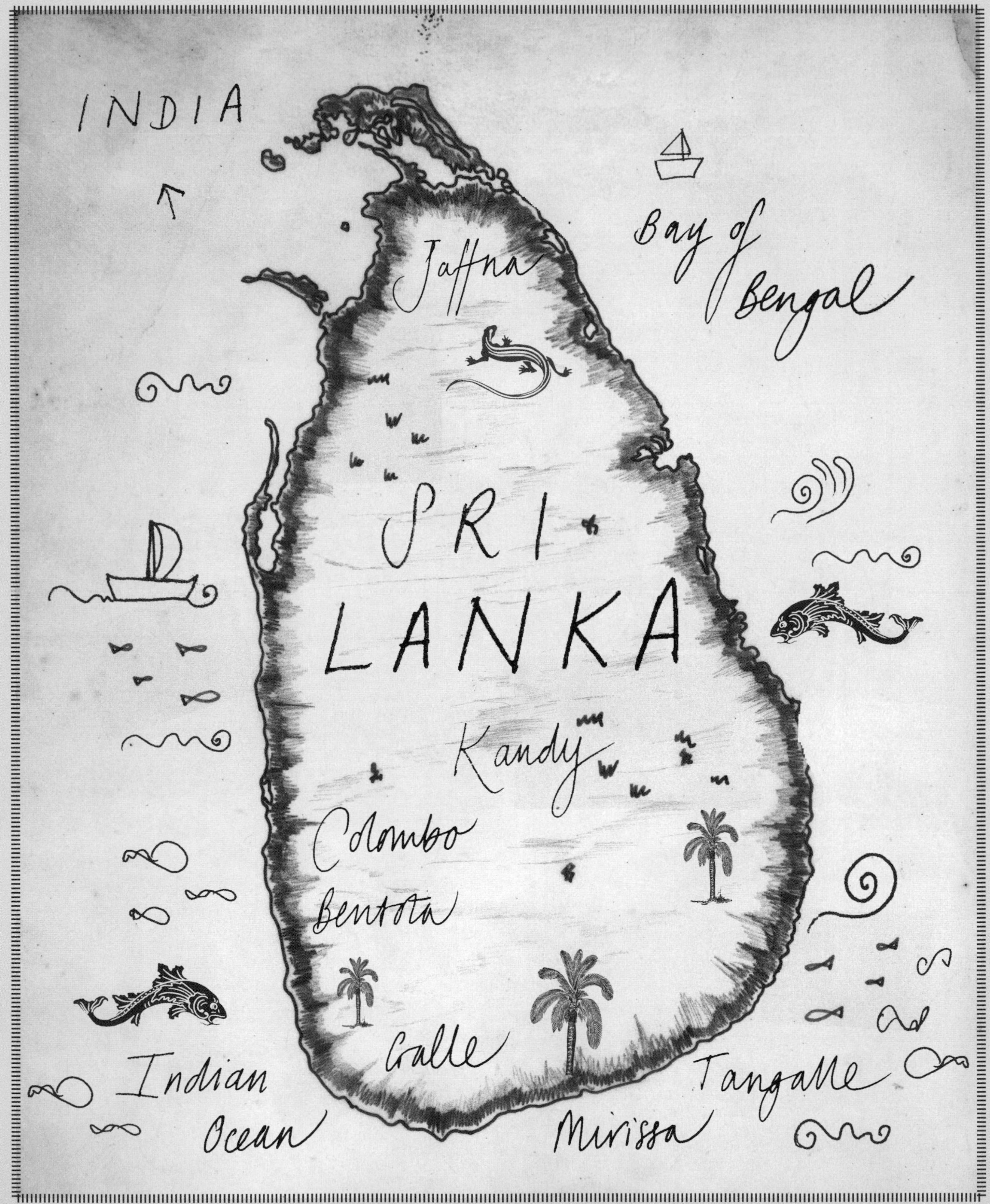

INDIA

Jaffna

Bay of Bengal

SRI LANKA

Kandy

Colombo

Bentota

Galle

Tangalle

Mirissa

Indian Ocean

Introduction

Just what is it that makes a great Sri Lankan home? This is the thorny question that the photographer James Fennell and I set out to answer on our three-month journey around the 'Paradise Isle', as Sri Lanka is justifiably known.

Despite its relatively tiny area – it is roughly the same size as the Republic of Ireland or West Virginia – Sri Lanka is a country of extraordinary contrasts. A fifteen-minute walk can take you from the beating sun of the salt pans to the breezy respite of the cinnamon hills. You can wake up sweltering on the coast and go to bed in the mountains, fervently wishing you had packed a sleeping bag and an extra pair of socks.

Buddhists (70%), Hindus (12%), Muslims (10%) and Christians (6%) are among the 22 million citizens who share the island, and their places of devotion and their icons – sometimes towering painted monuments, sometimes humble roadside shrines – stud the landscape, creating an overriding sense of tolerance and pluralism. In terms of buildings, relics of Dutch, Portuguese and British colonial architecture jostle for space alongside the best – and, it must be admitted, worst – of modern Asian design.

Creating this book was a challenging, but hugely enjoyable and rewarding experience. We travelled thousands of miles, tracing the palm-fringed coastline and criss-crossing the paddy fields, coconut groves and tea plantations of the interior on buses, trains, motorbikes, in taxis and the three-wheeler rickshaws known as tuk-tuks. When the roads became too rough to take us any further, we simply hitched up our sarongs and walked.

We visited around fifty properties – of which twenty-six, the very best examples, are featured in this book – shot thousands of images and interviewed dozens of owners, interior decorators, architects, stylists and designers in an attempt to capture the essence of elegant Sri Lankan living.

Accurate generalizations are virtually impossible in a country of such architectural and aesthetic diversity, but one can be made safely: Sri Lankan style is rooted in the tropical climate of this island nation. Houses must withstand long days of unrelenting sunshine and torrents of water descending from the sky at a moment's notice.

It is hard to comprehend the intensity of a Sri Lankan rainstorm until you have been in one. It is rather like standing in a waterfall, or underneath a ladder, from the top of which a malevolent goblin pours great buckets of water on you. The first warning that rain may be in the offing is the sight of people running. You rarely see anyone run in Sri Lanka – a most laid-back place – the rest of the time. But, to avoid a soaking, people sprint. They run to bring in cushions, lower the plastic covers that protect the passengers and back seats of the three-wheeler rickshaws, and get the washing under cover.

Sri Lankan architect Chelvadurai Anjalendran disapproves of such frenetic activity. He told me that in a well-designed tropical house, the last thing you should have to do is 'run around closing windows' whenever it is about to rain. As he points out, the simplest *ambalama*, as the thatched shelters that dot the paths and byways of the Sri Lankan countryside are known, can cope with the mightiest rainstorm without such fuss. Two houses by Anjalendran are featured in this book: the Crooked House (p. 18), his own home in Colombo, and Mount Cinnamon (p. 142).

Anjalendran was a student of – and is now an authority on – the most important and influential Sri Lankan architect of all time, Geoffrey Bawa. One of the most remarkable houses we visited was Claughton House (p. 32), which Bawa originally built in 1984 as a holiday home for a retired British gentleman, but is now owned by the American financial services executive Brian Brille. Inexplicably, Claughton is barely mentioned in the official histories of Sri Lankan architecture. It is therefore a great pleasure to feature Claughton in this book, as it is a masterclass in Bawa's contextual modernism, which set the stage for so much of what was to follow in Sri Lanka.

Rolling down the side of a steep hill towards the sea, Claughton does what all Sri Lanka's finest houses do: it skilfully blurs the line between inside and outside. At Claughton, you get all the benefits of being outside when you are inside (first and foremost, a cool natural breeze) and all the advantages of being inside when you are outside (shelter from the beating sun). The main living space – furnished with immovable concrete sofas, tables and benches, which are actually cast into the polished concrete floor – is built on three different levels, connected by steps and roofed by a giant pavilion. The levels, each a little more exposed to the elements than the last, cascade down the hillside, which itself rolls towards the original Bawa pool, before land surrenders to the cliffs and the sea. As James's photographs show, the house mimics, co-exists with and complements the surrounding landscape perfectly.

Claughton is such an interesting house for any serious student of Sri Lankan style because, while it arguably lacks the glamour of some of the architect's later buildings, it is Bawa in the raw, stripped down and supremely confident. These days, Bawa's influence – evident in concrete columns, lofty pavilions and cast latticework – is felt everywhere in modern Sri Lankan architecture, and his legacy is interpreted with varying degrees of success, from triumph to travesty.

One interesting and successful Bawa interpretation is Tittaniya (p. 136), the home of Irish expatriates Lisa Forde and Eric Ring. The house, near Galle's Wijaya beach, has Bawa's famous concrete pillars, but by the simple device of putting a 30-degree tilt on them, the owners have created a building that pulls off the rare feat of being fresh and simultaneously nostalgic. The couple built the house themselves, despite having no architectural training; Lisa is an interior designer, and Eric a rock musician. One cannot help thinking that Bawa, who had no formal training himself when he entered the profession (although he acquired some later on), would have approved.

Very few houses in Sri Lanka are old, in the way Europeans might think of an old house. There are only a handful of houses over a hundred years old in this book, and all have been extensively restored. The humidity, the sunlight and the relentless sea spray coming off the coast are to blame; they exact a heavy toll on any structure. After just five years, even a house that is meticulously maintained by a cadre of cleaners and painters can start to look tired. Glass in particular ages badly, becoming milky, and the wisest Sri Lankan architects avoid using a pane more of it than is absolutely necessary.

For similar reasons, even a millionaire's Sri Lankan house is likely to contain little in the way of valuable art. The climate is just too unforgiving on such work to risk it. Many art collectors keep their treasured pieces at homes in more temperate locations, such as London or New York. Some of the art collectors whose homes we visited, such as Oonagh Toner (p. 86) and Miles Young (p. 18), instead hang works by local artists, street artists and students in their houses. Celebrated indigenous artists such as Laki Senanayake, of course, are careful to work in media that can withstand the climatic demands of their homeland.

Similarly, rather than fill a room with expensive antique pieces from auction rooms, even the wealthiest home owners in Sri Lanka are forced to be more creative, enlivening simple pieces of furniture – often cast in concrete – with batiks, prints and artfully crafted cushions. Colour choices on the frequently expansive walls are critical. Flights of fancy can be taken with wooden furniture – note, for example, the wonderful four-poster beds that grace almost every bedroom in this book – as the items are usually made to order by local craftsmen, at prices that compete very favourably with the mass-produced alternatives available back home.

With the luxury of guaranteed sunlight, which barely moves throughout the year as the country is just a few hundred miles north of the equator, an even more creative way of decorating walls and floors is often found in the careful use of shadow. The play of light and dark is an integral part of every well-designed Sri Lankan home, as many of James's photographs illustrate. Slatted walls, for example, are often used not only to provide a permeable barrier to the outside world, but also to cast geometric columns of light and dark on corridors

and hallways. The intricate fretwork grilles traditionally found above grand entrances in the old *wallawwas* – as the colonial manor houses, such as the one restored by the actress Gillian Anderson (p. 44) in the hills outside Colombo, are known – are used to similar effect in the most stylish modern Sri Lankan houses.

The courtyard is the other great unifying concept of Sri Lankan homes. Courtyards work in Sri Lanka because they meet various practical and aesthetic needs. As they allow structures to be just 'one room thick', courtyards are essential for good ventilation in any sizeable house. High roofs keep the sun off the easy chairs and sofas invariably pushed up against the walls – although the mellower sun in the early morning and late afternoon can still warm one side of the courtyard, then the other.

Rain funnelled into internal courtyards is often collected in a fish or frog-filled pond, which lends a soothing and tranquil note. Many owners add an artistic network of guttering to create dramatic waterfalls, spouts and cascades of water that mesmerize the eye during a downpour.

The best Sri Lankan architecture acknowledges that it can never beat the weather; instead of attempting to lock out the heat and the humidity with banks of air conditioning, it engages in a coquettish dance with the elements. Massively high, overhanging roofs are the first line of defence against both rain and sun, but clever use of walls to create what architects call 'double screens' – two external walls close enough to each other to provide double the amount of shade – are also a feature. Another popular trick among Sri Lankan architects is the 'stack effect': by designing a room with one large opening and one small opening, thanks to the complicated physics of air buoyancy, you are rewarded with a natural light breeze at all times in the room.

Increasingly, these traditional methods of staying cool are being overlooked in favour of air conditioning, especially at beach properties, many of which need to be rented out to international tourists to pay for their upkeep. But in the mountains and at private houses, owners prefer to keep things as simple and – particularly given the high price of electricity in Sri Lanka – cost-effective as possible.

Since the publication of James Fennell's first book about the island, *Living in Sri Lanka* (2006), written with our friend Turtle Bunbury, who was unavailable to work on this book (lucky me!), huge change has swept through the country. Most of James's first book was shot before the devastating 2004 tsunami, which is estimated to have killed at least 30,000 people in Sri Lanka. This tragic event triggered extensive rebuilding and remodelling. Also notable are the political changes that have taken place in Sri Lanka since the end of the civil war in 2009, which have had an enormous impact. Peace has led to soaring domestic and international confidence in the country. While Western Europe has spent much of the last decade bumping in and out of economic recession, the economy in Sri Lanka has grown at an average pace of 6.5% a year.

While the Hong Kong banking and business high-fliers (especially expatriate Britons) have long prized Sri Lanka as a conveniently located tropical hidey-hole, the island is now experiencing a fresh influx of wealth – and energy – from the industrialists, commodity barons and internet entrepreneurs of Russia, China and India. Wealthy investors are bringing in world-class international architects, such as Japan's Shigeru Ban, the visionary behind the breathtaking Cliffhanger (p. 148), which clings precariously to the cliffs above Weligama Bay.

The rate of building is extraordinary. In places, it is clearly out of control – for example, the remote character of Mirissa and Weligama beaches has been utterly destroyed by the indiscriminate rush to throw up shoddy surf shacks and a wildly inappropriate high-rise hotel – but in other places, the injection of money is creating a vibrant and striking modern architectural style. This is an account of a nation in flux, a country busily and proudly reimagining itself as a connected, stylish and dynamic 21st-century playground, and we hope you will enjoy immersing yourself in this book as much as we enjoyed creating it.

Tom Sykes

TRADITIONAL

Traditional Sri Lankan architecture has two major advantages over more modern construction – lower electricity bills and no windows to clean. This is because the traditional Sri Lankan building eschews air conditioning (and the windows needed to keep that expensively generated cool air inside) in favour of more ancient cooling techniques. High vented roofs draw air upwards, creating a steady, light breeze, while courtyards provide sheltered outside seating areas throughout the day. Sri Lankans are also expert at the careful planting of magnificent tropical trees – palm, teak, jackfruit and mango, among many others – which provide another layer of shade.

In most traditional Sri Lankan houses, the kitchen is wood-fired and located outside. The advantages of having an outside kitchen are manifold: not only are smells and smoke kept away from the occupants of the house, but it is also the easiest way of ensuring that not a single joule of heat is released in the house itself. Wood-fired stoves, the purists claim, are also the best way to cook the traditional Sri Lankan dahl (lentil curry), which forms a staple of every meal. The smoke imparts a gentle extra aroma to the dish.

Many of the more remote settlements in Sri Lanka still subsist off the merest trickle of mains electricity, so at night you will often find your way lit by hundreds of flickering hurricane lamps (although, to watch out for snakes, a torch is also a must). Clothes are generally washed in the river and pressed with an iron fired with charcoal made from coconut husks, because electricity is either not available or prohibitively expensive.

That said, we also include some clearly very sophisticated buildings in this selection – and ones where electricity supply is not a problem – as a tribute to the way their owners have sympathetically renovated or built while respecting the local architectural vernacular.

THE CROOKED HOUSE

So named for the jagged shape of the plot it occupies, the Crooked House, in Colombo's Battaramulla district, is the product of one of Sri Lanka's most distinguished and celebrated architects, Anjalendran. The clever, compact house is shared by Anjalendran and Miles Young, the Hong Kong-based advertising executive who owns Mount Cinnamon (p. 142) in Mirissa, which was also built by Anjalendran. It draws inspiration from the British concept of a 'chummery' – a house in which three separate 'chums' could live both independently and communally. For Young, the house is a decompression chamber where he can stop off en route to and from Mirissa, and for Anjalendran – whose own full-time residence is just a few hundred yards away – the house is an art gallery for his impressive collection of indigenous, religious and contemporary art.

The feature that first strikes many visitors to the house is the inventive approach to colour, particularly the subtle use of three shades of blue, which lend depth and contrast to doorways, pillars and surfaces. The colour scheme was devised by the legendary Sri Lankan designer Barbara Sansoni (as Anjalendran freely admits, 'I have no idea about colour'). Anjalendran's principles are, however, to be found in every other detail of the building. One example is the trademark Anjalendran double-height ceiling, which creates a Bawa-like pavilion super-structure over the main living space. Another delightful aspect of this house is the collection of original Bawa furnishings that dot the rooms, such as the magnificent corrosion-resistant brass lamps.

As students of Anjalendran would expect, the philosophy of the house is rooted in mitigating the tropical weather. This means overhanging roofs (inspired by nothing more complex than the *ambalama* or rest pavilion) to keep out sun and rain, a minimum of glass and 'double screens' – two external walls close enough to each other to provide double the amount of shade. 'You often find in Sri Lanka that, however good a house looks in photographs, many architects don't even understand the basic climate conditions,' says Anjalendran. But, as he points out, you can sit in the Crooked House in the middle of the day and 'it is much cooler than outside'.

For Anjalendran, working on his own house was not much different from working on a client's house. He interviews his potential clients to see if he will consent to build a house for them, not the other way round. 'I have never believed the customer is always right,' he says firmly. 'I have sacrificed enough to know that. I did errands for Bawa for ten years, forty hours a week, for no pay, and the most important thing I learnt was to distinguish good from bad.'

But surely it must have been a relief to be freed from contracts and the other legal niceties that can so often get in the way of construction projects? 'I have never signed a contract in my life,' he says. 'You only get into contracts if you want to try and sue each other. You spend all your time not doing what you are supposed to be doing, but safeguarding yourself from litigation. I prefer trust. Fifty years ago, that was the normal way of doing things; you shook hands. People sold companies on a handshake. It is a different way of life, but a way of life I can still retain.'

Most of Anjalendran's professional career has been focused on the building of Sri Lanka's charitable SOS Villages and, as a result, frugality is deeply ingrained in his practice. 'I don't deal with rich people,' he continues. 'The idea that the purpose of architecture is to mollycoddle the rich is a lot of nonsense.'

It is suggested that, on leaving the Crooked House, the visitor does not compliment the great architect on his style. 'What is style?' Anjalendran says. 'I don't like style. Style is the opposite of great architecture. None of this is done to create a style. Style is when things don't work.'

The vibrant approach to the Crooked House shows the importance of colour choices in creating a welcoming urban–tropical space.

The ledge running along the upstairs balcony is the perfect showcase for Anjalendran's diverse collection of religious art, accumulated over several decades. The architect dislikes using glass, preferring to rely on natural ventilation and 'double screens' (two external walls) to keep it cool inside. The polished concrete floors recall the work of Anjalendran's former boss, Geoffrey Bawa.

Like many Sri Lankan homes, the Crooked House is furnished with locally made pieces of furniture. Although inexpensive by Western standards, these creations generally last only a couple of years owing to the high humidity in the general environment.

The double-height ceilings are an Anjalendran trademark. As well as creating a spacious tropical aesthetic, they provide natural ventilation, drawing hot air upwards. Externally, a towering roof with an enormous overhang is also the ultimate protection against Sri Lanka's torrential rainstorms.

Anjalendran is a master of simplicity, as this elegant upstairs bedroom shows to great effect.

left and opposite The use of colour – masterminded by Anjalendran's old friend, the Sri Lankan legend Barbara Sansoni – elevates the Crooked House entirely. The use of three well-considered shades of blue as the primary pigments throughout the house transforms door and window frames from workaday necessities into miniature works of art.

TRADITIONAL

THE KANDY SAMADHI CENTRE

Waruna Jayasinghe had always dreamed of being an architect. However, when he was only 23, his father fell sick and Jayasinghe was obliged to take over the family furniture business. Business was tough in those chaotic times, but Jayasinghe had a flair for making money, and he grew the enterprise steadily and surely. It eventually became what is today one of Kandy's best-known antique stores, Waruna Antiques.

The profits allowed Jayasinghe to return to his original dream of architecture. With the help of friends, he bought an abandoned tea estate about 45 minutes from Kandy. The site was in a notorious slice of bandit country, which perhaps explains why Jayasinghe paid just $20,000 for the stunning piece of mountainside in 1999 (it is now, like the rest of the country, at peace). An idyllic, steep-sided river runs through the property, where guests can spend many blissful hours rock-hopping their way upstream, swimming and experiencing the delights of sitting behind sheeting waterfalls. Compared to the city and the beach, it is delightfully cool at night, and entirely free from mosquitoes.

For the first thirteen years of his ownership of the estate, the single-minded Jayasinghe refused to travel, as he did not want his own ideas to be unduly influenced by the architecture he might see overseas. He started off by renovating the existing house on the hillside estate for his parents, and then built an extraordinary bachelor pad for himself, which boasts a gigantic boulder half-buried in the mud floor of the otherwise empty ground level.

'When I excavated the place I found this beautiful rock and I thought, "This is going to be my spiritual home,"' explains Jayasinghe. Accordingly, he has created an altar dedicated to icons and imagery of the major world religions in the mezzanine bedroom area upstairs: 'I love all the religions; I love Jesus, I love Shiva, I love Kali.'

Now that the 'difficult times have passed' with the end of the civil war, Jayasinghe has gently morphed into

a hotelier of sorts, and to house his guests he has built additional structures around the estate – fourteen at the last count – each as inventive and unique as the last. 'My lack of formal training actually made me bolder,' says Jayasinghe. 'I am not in a box; I can think in different ways.'

The focal point is the yoga and meditation hall. Here it is hoped guests may reach *samadhi*, an all-encompassing term describing absolute meditative absorption where, as Jayasinghe puts it, the 'third eye' of the mind is opened and one goes beyond the world of the five senses. Jayasinghe – who often rises at 3 a.m. to meditate and only 'returns to normal life' when he hears his wife and daughter stirring – describes *samadhi* as an otherworldly experience. 'When you deal with only the five senses, eventually you get bored,' he says. 'You want to get to a higher plane. I have this vision and I dream of higher states for all human life. I want to create somewhere for people to experience it.'

There could be no more inspiring place to begin that process than the Kandy Samadhi Centre.

opposite The special atmosphere at the Kandy Samadhi Centre is enhanced by the use of architectural salvage. Examples include the remarkable antique doors that dot the buildings of the estate, many of which were originally bought for sale in the owner's shop.

above A winding road runs through the Kandy Samadhi Centre, straddled by numerous outbuildings, including a forge and a laundry hut.

right A secluded seating area.

below Rough earth-brick walls create a feeling of deep connectedness with the planet at the Kandy Samadhi Centre. Traditional building materials and techniques have been used throughout, wherever possible. Authenticity was an important factor, but so was the knowledge that traditionally constructed buildings can withstand the rigours of the Sri Lankan climate.

opposite, above The Kandy Samadhi Centre makes a virtue of convenience with these rustic pillars, cut directly from trees on the estate. Using materials such as these to create new spaces for visitors was both cost-effective and inherently authentic to the traditional architectural vernacular.

opposite, below As an antique dealer, owner Waruna Jayasinghe is offered a constant flow of religious and indigenous antiquities, many of which have been artfully embedded into the fabric of the buildings, giving a unique and deeply personal slant to the Centre.

Power is in short supply up in the mountains, so instead Jayasinghe has to rely on ancient methods to keep cool – tiled floors, thick mud walls and lofty ceilings to provide shelter and shade. There are few mosquitoes at this altitude, but beds are equipped with nets to keep out the creepy crawlies that are part of Sri Lankan life.

Jayasinghe salvaged these short pillars from a fine house in Jaffna, which was torn down during the civil war. They were being transported to a bakery, where they would have been used to fire the ovens, when one of Jayasinghe's friends spotted them and saved them from the flames.

CLAUGHTON HOUSE

Constructed by the late, great Geoffrey Bawa, Claughton House, perched on a stunning clifftop above the crashing waves of Dikwella Bay, is a remarkable pavilion-like structure that seamlessly blends indoor and outdoor living in classic Sri Lankan style. The house was built for Richard Fitzherbert-Brockholes, an Englishman whose family seat, Claughton Hall in Lancashire, provided the name for his Sri Lankan fantasy. Fitzherbert-Brockholes had first discovered Sri Lanka in 1944, when he was evacuated to Colombo hospital from the Royal Navy ship on which he was serving, suffering from appendicitis. He started returning to Sri Lanka in the 1980s, and in 1984 he commissioned Bawa to build Claughton, where he spent the British winter.

Claughton is now in the proud possession of the American financial services executive Brian Brille, who bought the property after moving from New York to Hong Kong in 2009. His role covered twelve different countries, one of which was Sri Lanka. Struck by the friendliness of the people and the amazing diversity and potential of the country, Brille began what he describes as a 'systematic' hunt for the ultimate slice of oceanfront real estate with the help of a Sri Lankan colleague. The search eventually led him to the jewel that is Claughton House.

'There is so much that is appealing about Sri Lanka,' says Brille. 'The history, the ancient Buddhist civilizations, the rain forest, the tea country, the architecture, the infrastructure left behind by the British. And then there is Bawa. I grew up in a town right outside Chicago, and I always loved the work of Frank Lloyd Wright and the landscape architect Frederick Law Olmsted, and Bawa is very much of that ilk, that school. In so much of his work, and especially at Claughton, you really feel the lines of the building are an extension of nature. It is just an amazing place.'

Few would argue with that assessment. Although Claughton is undoubtedly a glamorous and hugely ambitious and impressive house, it also has the confidence to be utterly understated and unshowy. When arriving at the front of the house, for example, the modest, single-storey façade gives no suggestion of the multilayered flight of fancy that awaits on the other side of the walls.

The main living and dining area is a graduated, split-level space, and with each set of steps descended, one is gently propelled further and further outside as the sides of the house open up. However, the whole structure is very simply tied together by the lofty, overarching roof, panelled in weathered ceiling boards, and supported by blue wooden pillars reminiscent of the traditional Buddhist temples that dot the surrounding area.

The upper level is dominated by an enormous concrete table, cast into the fabric of the structure, which can seat ten with ease. Steps then lead down to a mezzanine level, which hosts a relaxed seating area, furnished again with cast concrete furniture, softened with comfy cushions and side lamps that evoke a colonial drawing room. Another set of steps leads down to the third, garden level, where plug sockets and the other accoutrements of a modern building disappear and the chairs are more reminiscent of garden furniture than a tea planter's sitting room. The magical 8-acre (3-hectare) garden then falls away from the edge of the floor pad, palm-studded greenery rolling down towards the original Bawa-designed pool and the ocean beyond.

With its stunning location, impeccable provenance and remarkable views, it is impossible to say that Claughton is anything other than one of the finest houses in Sri Lanka.

opposite The main pavilion is a stunning and unusual example of Bawa's work.

above The garden rolls down a steep slope to the ocean.

left It would be difficult to find a more inviting pool than this Bawa original, which boasts enviable views across the bay. The unconventional shape of the pool is complemented by the stylish geometric design under the water.

below The cast concrete table is on the highest of the three levels that make up the main living space of the central pavilion. Tucked away under the eaves, the table is well protected from rainstorms, making it an extraordinary space in which to read or write, or simply enjoy fresh fish from the ocean below, whatever the weather.

The simple pool shelter provides a perfect spot to relax with friends while soaking up the stunning beach vista. It will come as no surprise to students of Bawa that the furniture is made of durable cast concrete, softened with cushions.

Early morning sunlight casts striking patterns across the rough concrete floor of Claughton's garden level. The high pavilion roof ties together the disparate elements of the property with grace and style, making this one of the finest and most interesting houses in Sri Lanka.

above and left The air-conditioned, glazed bedrooms at Claughton emphasize simplicity and lean styling. The pictures on the walls are from Galle boutique Stick No Bills, which specializes in vintage Asian poster art, as well as producing retro-inspired, authentic prints of its own. The brightly coloured prints are popular throughout Sri Lanka, not least because many owners are reluctant to put high-value works on the walls for fear of damage.

TRADITIONAL
DUBU

George Cooper was on a shopping trip to Bali, where, he admits, he was only supposed to be buying benches. But one thing led to another, and he ended up buying this almost complete dwelling, and then exporting it back to Sri Lanka for rebuilding in the grounds of his hotel, Kahanda Kanda (KK), near Galle. Well, you know how irresistible it is when you see a real bargain.

The house in question is this sumptuously restored, 34 sq. ft (3 m²) *joglo*, as the traditional homes of high-status Javanese are known. After spotting it in the shop and being attracted by the intricately carved roof – 'I just looked up and there it was' – Cooper arranged its export back to Sri Lanka, and the hard work began.

'We wanted to create the wrap-around verandah, and we replaced many of the roof rafters with new ones, but the eaves were then in the sightline, so we had to effectively jack the whole building up and quite literally raise the roof,' says Cooper. 'It ended up being a bit more problematical than first envisaged.'

The *joglo* was originally open-sided, so walls were created using plain wood and then carpeted with woven palm panels to give a more rustic, artisanal feel. Outside bathrooms were added at the back of Dubu, as Cooper calls the *joglo*, with a small WC inside for night-time use. Dubu makes a striking exception to the overall aesthetic of Cooper's KK hotel, with a more traditional feel than many of the other buildings.

The use of a traditional Javanese house in Sri Lanka might strike some as unsympathetic to the culture of the island. However, Dubu is also a perfect latter-day representation of Sri Lanka's long history as a cross-cultural hub, receptive to and influenced by outside traditions. In terms of external influences on the country's architectural heritage, with the focus often on its colonial past, a structure such as Dubu shows that, with imagination, Sri Lanka is an entirely appropriate home for more tropical, indigenous traditions.

The *joglo* is, of course, perfectly engineered for a second life in Sri Lanka as the extremes of climate – bucketing rain, beating sun and balmy nights, depending on the season – are so closely mirrored in the country for which it was originally designed.

For all that, Dubu is a true one-off, even in a country that sometimes seems to be made up exclusively of one-offs. And, one must admit, a *joglo* is quite something to bring back from a routine shopping trip.

41

opposite Plain wooden floors and pared-down furnishings make Dubu an icon of simplicity and downsized living.

above The peaked roof of a *joglo* is a common enough sight in other parts of Asia, but Dubu is the only one of its kind to have been exported to Sri Lanka. Tucked away amid the greenery and tropical undergrowth of George Cooper's Kahanda Kanda hotel, the structure nonetheless blends sympathetically with its surroundings.

below Fans of George Cooper's distinctive modern take on classic British and colonial style will not be disappointed with the gorgeous and minutely considered interior of Dubu. With space at a premium, every stick of furniture is a thought-through indulgence.

right The magnificent fretwork in the panels above the windows is just one of the many remarkable details to savour in this immaculately restored Javanese cabin. The huge double bed, framed by handsome pillars, was specially commissioned for the space and had to be built in situ by local carpenters before the walls were erected around it owing to its titanic proportions.

TRADITIONAL
PILIMETENNE

Like many travellers, Hollywood actress Gillian Anderson fell in love with Sri Lanka the first time she visited the island. And, like many before her, she swiftly made the decision to buy a house there. Absolute and total privacy was an essential precondition, so house-hunting took her to numerous out-of-the-way, non-tourist locations. Eight months pregnant, she finally settled on an abandoned *wallawwa* near the small town of Pasyala, roughly halfway between Kandy and Colombo.

The house was well known – even revered – locally as it had been inhabited by a powerful and well-connected political family, but, by the time Anderson took it over, the once imposing *wallawwa* at the epic summit of a vast tea estate was in full-scale decline. 'The house hadn't been lived in for thirty years and was covered in mould and blackness and was literally falling apart,' says Anderson. There were a few dilapidated outbuildings, and one of these – four walls with no roof – was turned into the first habitable property on the estate, the Stone House, in which Anderson and her family stayed while the main house was being rebuilt.

The first order of business in the main house was relaying the floors, which were 'completely hacked up with chisels and sledgehammers, by hand, by men wearing flip-flops'. They were relaid using local timber and bespoke terrazzo, based on tiles found in the bathrooms.

The restoration of the shell of the structure, including the extraordinary curved upper balconies, which swoop around one side of the property like a heavenly reinterpretation of M.C. Escher, came next, and Anderson added and improved on many of the original features you see in these photographs, such as the peacock-inspired mouldings and the delicate plasterwork.

Some obstructive, turret-like structures were torn down and replaced with flat roofs, which have become magical seating areas, complete with simple, comfortable cushions and cast concrete benches. On one of these flat roofs, Anderson installed a healing mosaic of pebbles, which deliver a blissful massage to your feet as you walk on them.

The ground floor is dominated by a huge kitchen and living area, with an exquisite drawing room off to one side boasting what is surely one of Sri Lanka's most impressive ceilings, hand-painted with a striking lotus design by the celebrated Spanish artist Nuria Lamsdorff (who also created a bespoke range of china for the house). Guests can lie back on the comfortable vintage sofas and lose themselves in the swirling imagery for many hours.

It is the level of detail in the finishing, furnishing and fixtures that truly elevates the house. Spinning lazily in the afternoon heat, the gorgeous vintage fans from India are just one example (Anderson bought them on eBay, along with some of the light fittings). Among the quirkier features of the house are the metal hoops attached to one of the bedroom walls, which form a *Jack and the Beanstalk*-style vertical route to an elevated meditation area. 'I meditate, and I always create loft spaces,' explains Anderson. 'They are the ideal spot to unwind and truly relax.'

The garden is equally exquisite, and it is hard to believe that just a few short years ago it was an overgrown jungle. Now saved from destruction by Anderson's team, it even boasts a sacred tree from which the blossom can only be collected by specially ordained monks. It is just one more detail that confirms this house as one of the most remarkable in Sri Lanka.

45

opposite The internal rooms of Pilimetenne are linked by fabulous curved corridors, beautifully restored by Anderson's team of workmen and conservators in a veritable labour of love.

above The restored *wallawwa*.

The curved external walkway provides welcome respite from
the sweltering midday sun, and these seats, built into the fabric
of the structure, are a classic colonial touch – an ideal place to lie
back and doze away the afternoon.

Perfect for grand banquets or an intimate dinner with the family, the dining room is the beating heart of this house. Dramatic tropical flowers are freshly cut from the extensive grounds every day.

above The upstairs reading room is dominated by an archive chest, just one of many individual touches that render this home a truly exceptional discovery.

opposite The inspiring ceiling in the drawing room, designed and hand-painted over several months by Spanish artist Nuria Lamsdorff, is best viewed in a semi-prone position from one of the indulgent sofas below. The colourful, intricate design features lotus flowers, a recurring motif throughout the house.

below One of the joys of this house is the remarkable level of detail in the fixtures and fittings, such as this charming pendant lamp. Anderson bought many such items from eBay, including a selection of vintage fans from India.

right, above Anderson added this therapeutic mosaic when the house was being rebuilt and restored. As you walk barefoot around the rooftop installation, your feet are gently massaged by thousands of perfectly smooth stones – Zen-like contentment guaranteed!

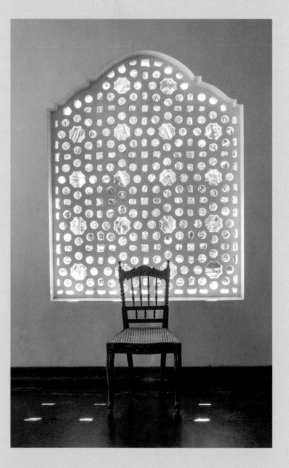

above Providing a permeable barrier to the outside world, exquisite peacock-inspired mouldings cast patterns of light on the floor below.

below The first-floor walkways follow the same elegant lines as those below, creating an effortless illusion of endless space throughout this magnificent property.

right The cast concrete bath is a truly indulgent addition. In colonial times, baths – or, more precisely, hot water – were a status symbol in Sri Lanka, and craftsmen still imbue them with magisterial dimensions that strain even the most efficient boiler.

TRADITIONAL
FIELD HOUSE

Rosamond Freeman-Attwood is the founder of Raison d'Etre, a consultancy and management company that has designed and run spas for five-star hotels all over the world. So it will come as little surprise that her own home, Field House near Galle, demonstrates extraordinary attention to detail, from the perfect internal courtyard to the sensitively chosen antiques and the idyllic shaded pool with its exquisite *ambalama* or rest pavilion, perfect for an afternoon nap.

Freeman-Attwood's route to calling Sri Lanka home is a typically circuitous one. Trained as a dancer and actor, she then worked as an alternative therapist in a clinic in the City of London. But several years of lugging massage tables round corporate offices in the city left her struggling with repetitive strain injury, and in 1999 she started Raison d'Etre, opening her first spa in the Maldives, together with a Swedish banker-turned-healer. They built more than sixty spas over the next few years, and won the global contract to many top brands, including Aman Resorts.

She consequently spent several months living in Galle, while setting up and training staff for Aman's two properties in Sri Lanka – Amangalla and Amanwella (pp. 80 & 192) – and became firm and fast friends with Olivia Richli, Amangalla's general manager at the time. It was Richli who inspired Freeman-Attwood to take the next step and find a Sri Lankan home of her own. One day, they were sitting in a bar on Wijaya beach when Richli pointed out that, around the table, Freeman-Attwood had all the people she would need to build a house in Sri Lanka, if she so chose: 'Olivia said, "He could help you find land, he could build it for you, he could be your project manager, and so on."'

A few days later, Eduard Hempel of Pearl Properties took Freeman-Attwood on a property tour. At house number four, she knew she had found her Sri Lankan home. 'It was just the verandah and the front rooms –

a tiny, tiny little house,' she says. 'The road wound down here, and it was full of roses and orchids, and I thought, "That's the kind of place I would like." I knew it was a "yes" immediately. It did take me about six months to actually say yes, because it was very scary.'

The redevelopment was managed by Oliver Francis. 'I couldn't have done it without him because I wasn't here very much,' Freeman-Attwood explains, 'and his taste is absolutely on a par with mine. It took two years to build.' Although she had originally intended to let the house out to holidaymakers once completed, Freeman-Attwood could not bring herself to do it in the end. She moved over lock, stock and barrel a few months after the house was finished. And really, who could blame her?

53

opposite The defining feature of this home is the stunning fish-filled pond at the centre of the internal courtyard. Water features are used to create a sense of inner peace and climatic respite, as well as providing a dramatic show when the rain gushes down.

above The front elevation of Field House is more or less unchanged from when the property was first built in 1910.

left Local craftsmen were tasked with making many of the fixtures and fittings, and items such as these shelves give Field House a more homely feel than many other properties. As a smaller dwelling, this house has a kitchen inside the main building.

below The clean, unfussy aesthetic of Raison d'Etre spas is recreated in this stylish living space. Note the apparently casual way that the pale washed blue of the shelves and drawers complements the floor panel in the same hue.

The rustic character of this shaded outdoor/ indoor social area is emphasized by a roughly hewn, oversized wooden table, with comfortable armchairs pulled up to make friends feel welcome and relaxed. The tiled floors continue unbroken from here into the house, creating a sense of unity, and tying together the inside and outside spaces – a vital quality in any authentic Sri Lankan home.

The house boasts a classic internal courtyard, allowing it to be 'just one room thick', so that all the bedrooms and living spaces can be ventilated from both sides. The gorgeous pillars holding up the roof structure are thought to have been salvaged from a property in the north of the country. The antique patina successfully masks the fact that this whole area is newly built.

This cosy space has all the comforts of
an inside living room – a comfy sofa, coffee
table, bookcases – but extends into the open
internal courtyard.

left and opposite The pool area has to be one of the most relaxing in Sri Lanka. Although the pool is small, its location, right on the edge of a paddy field, is unparalleled. The *ambalama* is simple but equipped with cushions and a squishy mattress, ideal for afternoon naps. As the pool is surrounded by lush vegetation, it remains refreshingly cool throughout the day.

below This elegant bedroom encapsulates the overall aesthetic of homely luxury that informs every square foot of Field House. The bathroom is hidden by the screen at the head of the four-poster bed, which is complemented by carefully selected antique furniture imported from abroad.

TRADITIONAL
37 LIGHTHOUSE STREET

Karl Steinberg built 37 Lighthouse Street backwards. He had bought a plot of land in the middle of Galle Fort, where he suspected an old Dutch merchant's house had once stood (before being illegally cleared and replaced with a modern horror), with the firm intention of creating something 'truly Dutch, really respecting that heritage and tradition', to use his own words. But, as is often the way in Sri Lanka, things did not progress at quite the speed anticipated. 'We got that piece of land, but for a long time it just sat there,' says Steinberg.

Owing to his local fame as the creator of the iconic and immaculately restored Galle Fort Hotel (in 2007 the property was given a UNESCO award for heritage conservation), Steinberg was frequently offered antiques by local dealers. 'One day I got the chance to buy a full set of 18th-century Dutch windows and doors, and a complete set of extremely rare satinwood grilles,' says Steinberg. 'I didn't really know what I would do with them, but they were too good to pass up, so I bought them.'

He continues: 'Then, a few months later, I was in Colombo and another dealer I knew said, "I have these very unusual 18-ft columns – you should come and take a look at them." I really didn't want to buy any 18-ft columns, but I ended up going, and the columns were just remarkable. They were huge, with an Indian influence, from northern Sri Lanka, and the wood was a wonderful piebald colour. So I bought them too.

'Then a guy came to the door of the Galle Fort Hotel with six terracotta tiles. They were clearly original Dutch tiles from the 1700s, and he wanted 30 cents for each of them. I said, "How many have you got?" And he said, "About 1,000." So I bought them too.

'So now I had the tiles, the pillars, and the windows and grilles. Sometimes you get the sense that a house is asking you to build it, and that's exactly what happened here. If you are a conservator, or work in that area, building is actually not so much about what you want. You have

to listen to the building, and it will tell you what it wants. That's how you capture the spirit of an architectural time when an entire group of people blossomed.'

So Steinberg set to work creating this magnificent and historically accurate property, knitted together by those grand pillars, which support the cathedral-like ceiling of the main *zaal*, as many owners still call their sitting rooms. His hunch that all this was meant to be was justified in remarkable fashion as they were putting the finishing touches to the house: 'The last thing we built was the front verandah. As we dug down, we discovered the original door stone – and it was exactly the same width, to within an inch, of the door we had bought.' This door stone is the last step before you hit the street. If you look carefully at the picture above, you can still see the marks where the original pillars would have stood.

But there was another, even more phenomenal surprise to come. 'We found a number of tiles that were exactly the same as the 1,000 Dutch tiles we had bought,' says Steinberg. 'Most were broken, but five of them were intact. So we took those five and laid them right in the middle of all the others.'

Karl and his partner now spend as much time as possible in Galle Fort. 'Birds and butterflies fly in and out, and squirrels and monkeys steal your breakfast,' says Steinberg. 'The house does respect the historical traditions of the Fort – but it's also the most fabulous place to live.'

opposite A stylish bench casually pushed up against the shutters provides the perfect place to relax.

above The front verandah, featuring the original door stone of the Dutch house that once stood on this site.

opposite Steinberg's home is focused around this extraordinary double-height living area. While he was passionate about creating an authentic building in tune with the Dutch heritage, this is also a full-time home, and as such needs to be comfortable and inviting.

above The imposing pillars that dominate this dramatic central space are testament to an architectural mind obsessed with attention to detail. The delightful tile floor, elegant central light fitting and carefully selected antique furniture all add to the overall sense of culture and sophistication.

In Sri Lankan homes, outside
space is often as important as
the interior. With space at a
premium in Galle Fort, mirrored
windows are used to make
this outside area seem bigger.
Cast concrete furniture is also
remarkably space-efficient.

The traditional columns supporting the roof of the verandah lend an imposing, magisterial feel to this immaculately restored property. Steinberg's previous venture in Galle was given a UNESCO award for heritage conservation, so the quality in every inch of his own home will come as no surprise to those who know him.

above These versatile shutters revolve on an axis, allowing the wood-panelled living space to extend seamlessly into the courtyard when the shutters are open. The gorgeous table is a one-of-a-kind classic, with legs made from the antlers of a deer.

opposite, above The house is very much conceived around outdoor living, and these chairs (top right) offer a perfect view onto the courtyard. The exposed staircase leads to a verandah (top left), where rooms have glazed windows and air conditioning to ensure a restful night's sleep.

opposite, below The central courtyard may look like it has been here for a hundred years, but it was in fact a building site not that long ago – more proof of the incredible attention to detail that is characteristic of the house as a whole.

TRADITIONAL

MALABAR HOUSE

A visit to Galle Fort is an essential part of any trip to Sri Lanka. Dating from the Dutch colonial era and lovingly restored by owners David Salt and Katrina Wilson, Malabar House is one of the most charming properties in the Fort. The couple have retained the Moorish feel of the four-bedroom house, and the thick, whitewashed stone walls create a deliciously cool ambience – most notably in the reception hall, which gives on to a stunning courtyard with a bijou plunge pool for cooling off, exactly what you need after a hard day walking the historic ramparts.

The house has also been filled with a beautiful selection of antiques by the current owners, which perfectly complement the historic ambience of the very fabric of the building. Malabar House does not quite go back to the very earliest days of Western civilization here (the Fort itself was begun by the Portuguese, shortly after their first landing in the early 16th century), but this quintessential Galle Fort abode probably dates from some time between 1750 and 1775, when the Dutch era was at its peak, and the building of the public administration buildings, the Protestant church, the warehouses and residential quarters for wealthy merchants was undertaken.

The defensive mentality of the Dutch settlers is more than evident in the fortifications of Galle Fort, but the great advantage of a fort such as Galle was that houses no longer had to resemble medieval keeps: with security assured by the defences erected by the colonial companies, the settlers could make houses that were temples to sophistication and refinement. At Malabar House, this is apparent in the high doors and the handsome (but insecure) windows facing the street, which speak of an incredible confidence in the security apparatus of the city surrounding the first occupants of this house.

Galle was known to be the most civilized and salubrious city in the colonies thanks to an ingenious system of sewers that flooded at high tide, taking waste out to sea twice a day. A house as grand and important as Malabar would certainly have been connected to that system.

Today, Galle Fort is enjoying a remarkable renaissance. Just as the arty, ex-public-school boho set flocked to Marrakesh (and then spread out into the surrounding hinterland) in the 1950s and '60s, so a similar invasion is now taking place in this historic walled city. Described by one habitué as being 'more socially exclusive than Gloucestershire', Galle Fort is now home to a dizzying array of characters who would not be out of place in a novel by Nancy Mitford. Prime houses in Galle Fort regularly change hands for upwards of $5 million these days – an unthinkable figure even a few years ago.

But walking the streets of Galle Fort is to experience only half of the city: as in the great souks of Arabia, a whole world lies hidden in the courtyards behind those front doors. Malabar House is a perfect way into that once and still rarefied other existence.

Owing to its sheltered position, the plunge pool at Malabar House remains remarkably cool during the day and is the perfect place for sunbathers on the balcony above to let off steam.

The owners of Malabar House have furnished the property with a sophisticated blend of antique furniture, tribal art, metalwork and locally sourced craft items. The cool white walls and ceilings make this house a welcome retreat from the beating sun at any time of the day.

above, left The colonnaded walkway along the edge of the plunge pool gives a wonderful feeling of space. Note the thickness of the walls, which help to keep the house naturally cool.

top The owners of this relatively compact city home have maximized space, for example by installing built-in bunk beds in one of the smaller rooms.

above Another single bedroom is simply furnished with pale shades to emphasize coolness.

opposite The fabulous tapestry hanging on the wall above the sofa is a vibrant burst of colour in a landscape otherwise dominated by pale and pastel shades.

BHUDT FARM

In 1997, Jack and Jo Eden visited Sri Lanka on holiday and fell in love. The effect was so dramatic that, within a couple of months, they had both packed in their jobs in Hong Kong and relocated to Galle. They spent the next few years in Galle Fort and established what is still the country's pre-eminent luxury villa management service. Eden Villas now manages many of Sri Lanka's most exclusive properties.

Having lived in Sri Lanka for so many years, the Edens were often asked whether they knew of any houses for sale. Thus it was that Jack found himself taking a couple of potential buyers to see one dilapidated property sitting on a one-acre (0.5-hectare) promontory – an island – that juts out into the paddy fields just outside Galle. 'I began to show a few people this one, and on each occasion the house and land grew on me some more,' says Jack. 'It was in need of some loving, and the gardens were overgrown and unkempt, but I immediately enjoyed its setting.'

So the Edens bought it themselves. The purchase was complex because the man who had originally owned the land had left it to his two sons. They had divided the land equally, with the older son keeping the main house (which is about seventy-five years old) and the younger one building a new house on the other half-acre. But in the end the Edens acquired the whole plot and set to work renovating both houses and the gardens, levelling and extending the lawns and clearing jungle to reveal a wonderland of long-choked trees, including mango, rambutan, mangosteen, avocado, banana, jackfruit, jambu, kithul palm, papaya, pomelo, guava, clove, pineapple, breadfruit and king coconut.

They called the house Bhudt Farm after the Sinhalese word for 'cooked rice', a reference to the paddy fields that hug the boundary. 'We created a border with the construction of a dry-stone wall that now goes around the whole property,' says Jack. 'In places it is 6 ft high and 3 ft thick, and it is made of locally cut granite.

The mason who built it worked alone and placed each stone by hand.'

After years of living in Asia, the Edens have taken on board feng shui by osmosis, and have tried to use these principles wherever possible within the space. On a practical level, this involved removing interior walls, moving doorways to places that allowed a more natural flow, and creating windows to allow more light and air. One of the great joys of the house, Jack says, is to throw open the east-facing shutters at the break of dawn and witness the morning mist lift off the paddy fields with the rising sun.

The clever and compact kitchen space is notable for the ceiling racks from which a mind-boggling assortment of jugs and saucepans hang, in the unlikely event that guests feel like cooking for themselves rather than taking advantage of the couple's chef, widely reputed to be one of the best in Sri Lanka.

However, it is the main living area, with its eclectic pair of centuries-old Eden family portraits, that really catches the eye. The classic tropical design – wooden shutters, clay-tile steps, distressed wood, painted colours, smooth textures – dramatically contrasts with the appearance of the oil-painted ancestors, peering down sternly from the wall space. They survive the humidity but need regular cleaning and careful protection from less predictable threats. 'My greatest fear for them actually is from chipmunks that might nest behind them, and so to counter this I have placed the paintings several inches away from the walls and am constantly checking for incursions,' says Jack.

75

opposite The chunky limewashed timbers of this double bed contrast beautifully with the finely detailed lines of the side table and chair.

above The property is situated on a promontory that juts out into paddy fields just outside Galle.

left The outdoor seating area is essentially an extension of the inside. The flooring, which runs continuously throughout the whole property, both inside and outside, helps to blur the lines between these two spaces in classic Sri Lankan style.

below British country farmhouse meets tropical necessity in the informal breakfast area, creating a relaxed, cool eating space.

Continuing the country farmhouse theme, pans and cooking implements hang down from the rafters. Were it not for the pineapples on the sideboard and the view over fields of palm trees, this could be mistaken for a cottage in the heart of England.

above The simple furnishings
in this children's bedroom
reflect the informal atmosphere
of the house as a whole.

right In the main living
area, the owners' forebears
gaze down from the walls
in all their historical finery,
contrasting dramatically with
the modern tropical design
and lending further character
to this unique property.

TRADITIONAL
AMANGALLA

Amangalla in Galle Fort started life as a Dutch barracks, but in 1863 it became Asia's first Western-style hotel when a consortium of British businessmen acquired the building and refitted it as the New Oriental Hotel. The New Oriental Hotel prospered, offering Western comforts to merchants and government officials in transit, most of whom were coming off the steamer that made a weekly stop in the prosperous fortified city. The hotel became a byword for the height of luxury.

But Galle was, in the century that followed, steadily eclipsed by Colombo, and the city's decline as a trading hub was mirrored in the fate of the New Oriental Hotel. Until 1995 it was held together by seemingly little other than the force of the will of the last family owner, the redoubtable Nesta Brohier. But after she passed away, the property began crumbling at an ever faster rate and seemed destined for an ignoble end. By February 2003, when the New Oriental Hotel finally closed, it had become so run-down, locals say, that the only thing you could order was a bottle of Lion beer, or alternatively be taken on a tour of the garden for 100 rupees.

Enter, on a white steed, the Aman group, which bought the property and comprehensively restored the hotel to a level of indulgence that those long-departed colonialists could only have dreamed of. Now the hotel – renamed Amangalla – is once again among the most luxurious and sophisticated in Asia.

Remarkably, the refitting has been achieved without compromising the character of the original structure. At the heart of the property is still the Great Hall or *zaal*, as it was known in colonial times. This entry point to the hotel has a wonderful old-world ambience with high ceilings, overhead fans and chandeliers, and an endless array of characterful pieces of furniture. There is also seating on the wide verandah facing the tree-lined street, an ideal place to escape the heat of the day and relax with a tall, cool drink.

Throughout the light-filled property, hotel staff – some of whom have been working there since Brohier's day – click their heels on the original, restored 300-year-old polished teak and jackwood floors. All the rooms – which overlook either the hotel gardens or Galle's Groote Kerk (Great Church) – are appointed with a four-poster king-size bed, writing desk, dining table, planter's chair, wardrobe and *pettagama* chest. Many pieces of furniture are original items from the New Oriental era, while the rest are careful reproductions. The cool, climate-controlled library at Amangalla houses a wonderful collection of books, photo albums and comment books for amateur historians interested in recalling the glory days of the New Oriental Hotel.

However, the jewel in the crown of Amangalla is undoubtedly the extraordinary Garden House, a bijou, self-contained two-storey cottage located down winding paths, among the palm and jackfruit trees that make up the hotel's peaceful gardens. Frequently rented as a honeymoon suite, this house was built specially by Brohier for one of her closest male friends with whom she enjoyed a long and enduring relationship, the exact status of which remains to this day shrouded in mystery.

opposite The restoration of this famous landmark reflects the aesthetic of the building as it was in the 19th century, although it dates back to the 17th century.

above Set within the walls of historic Galle Fort, Amangalla is an iconic emblem of the city.

The idyllic pool is the perfect place for travel-weary guests to kick back, relax and enjoy a cool drink from the bar.

The outside seating area of the Garden House, a secluded two-storey hideaway within the gardens, creates a world within a world at this celebrated hotel.

Former owner Nesta Brohier built the Garden House for one of her closest male friends. Although the status of their relationship remains a mystery, the romantic story of the house has inspired generations of travellers, and the space remains perhaps one of the most enchanting on the island.

TRADITIONAL
TALARAMBA REEF

One of the largest villas in Sri Lanka, able to sleep sixteen in comfort in eight double bedrooms, Talaramba Reef is understandably popular for big parties. The reason for its enormous capacity is that the property actually comprises two near identical villas – Villa Sulanga and Villa Vatura, each with its own pool – built side by side. The villas are connected with a stunning art-filled colonnade, which, while undeniably and unapologetically modern, also recalls classic Sri Lankan colonial design.

The two expatriate owners, Sarah Pringle and Oonagh Toner, are best friends and avid art collectors, and they make a habit of choosing new and exciting artworks by local up-and-coming artists to decorate the house. Witness gazelle heads made out of old motorbike handlebars, scrap metal fashioned into mesmerizing wall pieces, and inspiring paintings thoughtfully hung throughout both houses.

The local beach, whose waves you can hear crashing onto the shore at the end of the garden, is more suitable for walking and rock-hopping than swimming, but it has one very remarkable attribute – it is a turtle hatchery. Five of the world's species of turtle nest on Sri Lankan beaches, and if you wander quietly down here at night, there is every chance you may witness a 'juvenile frenzy', as hatchlings make their perilous first journey to the sea. In the daytime, you may be lucky enough to see larger turtles surfing on the waves of the reef.

For swimming and surfing, gorgeous Mirissa beach with its amazing waves and established swimming spots is just a few minutes away by tuk-tuk or, for those in search of a more colourful experience, an exhilarating 20-cent bus ride. Mirissa is also one of the best places in the world to see blue whales, and regular whale-watching trips depart from the pier.

The houses themselves are modelled along classic colonial lines – airy sitting rooms open to the elements on both sides, a restful pond in the central courtyard and fully air-conditioned bedrooms with en-suite bathrooms and wide balconies on both sides upstairs.

The villas are set in 2.5 acres (1 hectare) of lush tropical gardens. The steady sea breeze and the hypnotic sound of the Indian Ocean rolling onto the reef make this a very special place to do little more than unwind and reconnect with the simpler things in life.

opposite From this long colonnade, it is immediately apparent that the house is owned by art collectors. Many pieces, such as the fantasy animal head on the far wall, are made from pre-corroded metal (in this case, salvaged from motorbike parts).

above There is no shortage of seating options at this vast double villa, from squishy sofas to these elegant custom-made teak and wicker chairs.

The bedrooms all pursue a lean and sophisticated contemporary aesthetic.

Breakfast of fresh fruit and locally made
curds is served on the spacious verandah.

TRADITIONAL

THE MUDHOUSE

When Tom Armstrong went to work for three months as a volunteer teacher in the regional town of Anamaduwa in 1999, things did not turn out quite as planned. There were only four weeks of term left, the family he was living with were strictly religious and did not approve of him leaving the premises without being chaperoned by them and then, midway through the placement, he was dumped by his girlfriend back home. He went out to drown his sorrows with a friend, Ranjit Kumar, and they wound up by a stunning lake on the edge of town, where they resolved to buy a patch of land and build a cross between a holiday house and a den – an insane plan at the time as Anamaduwa was claimed by the Tamil Tigers.

It was 2004 before Armstrong and Kumar actually started building. With no money for materials, they did what the locals have been doing for millennia: the floors were made of compacted termite mud and dung, they built the frame out of rough, salvaged timbers, the rain and sun were kept off with palm thatch and the walls were built with mud bricks. They called it their mudhouse. Then came the tsunami, and they both downed tools for several months to help with relief efforts along the coast.

These days, the Mudhouse – the name stuck – comprises four extraordinarily original, light and airy high-ceilinged mudhouses, each built in a unique style, together with a variety of communal and staff outbuildings, sensitively nestled in 50 acres (20 hectares) of the evergreen dry-zone forest, about 100 miles (160 km) north of Colombo. The surrounding forest is rich in birdlife, with kingfishers, egrets and herons among the 100-odd endemic and migratory bird species in residence at any one time. Dawn chorus walks, led by the Mudhouse's local staff, are one way to experience the birdlife; another is simply to lie in bed and listen to the sounds of the jungle waking up around you.

There is a mere trickle of mains electricity to the office at the entrance to the Mudhouse, so at night the paths and

huts are lit by hundreds of flickering hurricane lamps (one employee, headquartered in the lantern hut, has the full-time job of maintaining the lights) and clothes are pressed with an iron fired with charcoal made from coconut husks in the laundry hut. Showers are cold, but flushable toilets are one luxury the Mudhouse does extend to.

Owing to the nature of the materials used – and, as Armstrong freely confesses, their lack of experience – the first structures on the site lasted only a few years, but as Armstrong and Kumar's building skills have improved, so has the expected lifespan of the huts. Building can take as little as a month once the decision to create a new hut is made and materials have been foraged. Indeed, the family hut was built after Armstrong accidentally accepted an overbooking. Not wanting to turn the group away, he and Kumar set about building a hut for them instead.

The latest development has been the acquisition of a new block of land to the north of the main site, containing an ancient 'tank', as the old Sinhalese reservoirs are known. Having been meticulously restored, it now not only feeds water to the farm, where produce is grown for the Mudhouse kitchen, but also provides private swimming and kayaking for guests. The high-ceilinged conical yoga hut, which stands on an island in the middle of the tank, makes an eye-catching focal point.

While clearly a fantasy, the Mudhouse's greatest achievement is that it never feels like a theme park. Instead, thanks to the entirely organic way in which the Mudhouse has grown up, the good-humoured attitude that pervades the place and the true 50/50 partnership between Armstrong and Kumar, the fabric of this remarkable jungle hideaway is shot through with an unmistakable authenticity of spirit.

The cavernous inside of one of the traditionally built huts (right); fresh flowers and fruit from the Mudhouse gardens (left).

above This stunning yoga hut was built on a natural island in the restored tank – as the ancient reservoirs of Sri Lanka are known – which now forms part of the Mudhouse estate. Guests are encouraged to make full use of the lake, which provides irrigation for the farm while doubling as a swimming pool.

opposite, above There are bicycles dotted around the Mudhouse grounds for guests to use.

opposite, below The traditional hanging chairs work perfectly in these dramatic spaces, most of which were built by owners Tom Armstrong and Ranjit Kumar, together with their friends and staff.

above There is no mains electricity in most of the properties on the Mudhouse grounds, so the lantern house is a vital facility.

opposite, above left Fresh fruit and vegetables in the kitchen.

opposite, above right Lunch can be served in the yoga hut, with a fantastic view of the tank beyond.

opposite, below Without electricity, cooking at the Mudhouse is done the old-fashioned way and tastes all the better for it.

The use of local materials, often salvaged from the bush, has led to these fantastic and dramatic living and sleeping spaces. The open roofs layer on top of each other, providing shelter from the sun and rain, but also allowing a chimney effect to draw air through the structures, which creates a steady breeze for the occupants and makes the spaces surprisingly cool and airy.

CONTEMPORARY

Contemporary design is increasingly making its mark in Sri Lanka as owners and architects seek to blend the amenities and comforts of the modern world with the charm and authenticity of this richly diverse island. The homes featured in this section bring a 21st-century aesthetic to the Sri Lankan experience.

Yet it is noticeable that even with air conditioning, modern kitchens and Western-style bathrooms and showers, the demands of the Sri Lankan environment and climate still reign supreme. So gigantic verandahs, huge, shade-giving roofs and lush, jungle-style planting co-exist with the clean lines and open spaces of the contemporary look. One of Sri Lanka's magical qualities is its ability

to draw from many different influences. Where else could contemporary design embrace the notion of having a live tree rising majestically through the interior of the house (pp. 106 & 120)?

Bawa is frequently indicted for the fetishization of concrete in Sri Lanka, but it must be said that it is a remarkably convenient material for what many people are seeking to achieve in modern Sri Lankan homes. Almost all of these striking contemporary houses, for example, feature cast concrete columns and polished concrete floors. If you did this in rainy Somerset, it would look horrendous. For some reason, in the heat and jungle of Sri Lanka, it looks – and feels – amazing.

The issue faced by contemporary houses is that they age quickly, and full redecoration is needed at least every three years to keep them looking wonderful. For every house featured here, we saw another three that had not been maintained well enough – milky walls of glass, sticky from sea spray, are the number-one offender, followed by out-of-control gardens that blot out the sun and the view. A large Sri Lankan garden produces quite literally tons of growth every year and needs to be cut back regularly.

But when they work, and when they are loved and lavished with time, money and attention, contemporary Sri Lankan houses – as the following pages show – are the best in the world.

CONTEMPORARY

IVORY HOUSE

Paul Walters and Tony Bannister are nothing if not a jet-set couple. Walters, an Australian by birth who has lived in Bali, Mexico, Hong Kong and Thailand, is the manager of a luxury hotel in London's West End, while Bannister, a Brit, runs his own global trend-forecasting company, dividing his time between Sydney and London. So these two are used to skipping around the globe sniffing out the hottest and hippest ideas, brands and places.

Hardly surprising, then, that when Aman Resorts opened in Sri Lanka in 2005, the pair booked themselves in for a ten-day stay. It was, says Walters, 'the perfect excuse' to visit the country. They were sufficiently impressed by Sri Lanka on their first trip that they looked at property for sale in the course of their visit. When they saw a small plot a few miles inland surrounded by paddy fields and palm trees, it was love at first sight. There was an old colonial house on the plot, but it was in a bad state of disrepair.

'What we were supposed to do was not make up our minds and go back home, and in the cold, hard light of day realize that it was just an impossible fantasy. But we didn't do that,' says Walters. Instead, a few months later, they were the proud owners of what would become the Ivory House: 'It didn't have any grandeur. It was a tiny Dutch house and basically we stripped it back to the bare bones and then built the house around the skeleton.'

Walters and Bannister retained the colonial feel – for example, the perfectly shaded 9-ft-wide (3-m) verandah where they eat all their meals – but overlaid the tea-planter look with a cool, contemporary aesthetic. The coolness of the cavernous sitting room, polished concrete floors and white walls is cleverly offset by the warmth of several European antique pieces, such as the dresser in the kitchen and the old chest of drawers in the sitting room.

The garden is simple and clean, in keeping with the aesthetic of the house – a gravel drive, palm trees and an azure pool – and a family of wild monkeys lives in the tops of the palm trees. In the magical hours of the early morning, as the mist rises off the paddy fields and the community around the Ivory House wakes up, the garden is alive with birdsong.

Walters and Bannister go to the Ivory House a minimum of twice a year, and love having guests to stay. 'We designed the house so it is the perfect place to have friends. There are as many bathrooms as there are bedrooms, so nobody has to share and all that sort of thing,' says Walters.

The project took them about three years from start to finish. The pair had a clear 'joint vision' and did without the services of an architect or interior designer in creating the Ivory House.

opposite A stunning blend of old and new, the Ivory House is one of the most elegant contemporary houses in Sri Lanka. Through the application of pale paint, the restored traditional grille above the door becomes a harbinger of modernity and, with the doorway, forms a perfect frame through which to view this well-considered abode.

above Low-slung modern sofas and pale walls make the most of the space and height of this lovingly restored and rebuilt Dutch colonial planter's house.

The dining area at the Ivory House is relaxed and informal. Everything in the house, from the artworks on the walls to the richly varied furniture, both modern and antique, was hand-picked by the discerning owners. The simple glass lightbulbs are practical on dark evenings, but also emphasize the minimalist aesthetic of the property.

above The bedrooms at the Ivory House indulge a more traditional vision of luxury than is found elsewhere in the property, with lavish four-posters and floor-to-ceiling shutters. The elegant furnishings ensure, however, that the contemporary feel of the home is not overly disrupted.

right The kitchens in many Sri Lankan houses are divided from the main house, but here the high-spec kitchen has been incorporated into the living space. Although attended by a fabulous full-time chef, Sunil, the accessible cooking area also telegraphs a clear message that the owners of this house are not above interrupting their holiday to boil their own egg. The black overhead lights provide pleasing points of visual contrast.

above The walkway leading to Walatta hints at the remarkable appropriation of living plants to be found in the fabric of the building.

left (from left to right) An outdoor seating area; a view of the sea; items from the owner's art collection.

THE WALATTA HOUSE

In 2000, the journalist and broadcaster Teymoor Nabili was looking for two things: a holiday home and a good investment. 'I was living in Singapore working as a business journalist at the time, and I wanted a place for holidays and I also wanted to invest. I didn't want to buy a place in Singapore, and I couldn't afford Bali. You always try to buy low and sell high, and from an investment perspective, nothing was lower than Sri Lanka in 2004. No one wanted to come here, but I had a look around and I thought it was an amazing opportunity. The beaches were incredible, and in 2002 the prime minister, Ranil Wickremesinghe, had signed a peace deal with the Tamil Tigers, which appeared to be holding.'

Nabili put his money where his mouth was and bought a 3-acre (1.2-hectare) clifftop site a few miles from the town of Tangalle. He was soon in the grip of a bad case of buyer's remorse. First, the civil war restarted; then, after the tsunami, all beachside developments were banned. 'The land was basically worthless,' he recalls. Like any good investor, however, Nabili played the long game, and in 2009, when the war came to an end for good, and building restrictions were lifted, he set about constructing the Walatta House.

Nabili – who is of Iranian and English parentage, and whose first name is an Iranian version of Tamburlaine – wanted to build something truly original and stumbled on the work of tropical architect John Bulcock while reading an architectural magazine. They decided to build something bold and modern and very different from what generally exists in Sri Lanka. 'The local aesthetic is nice,' says Nabili, 'but everybody was doing similar things, building in the same kind of language and vernacular. When I met John Bulcock, we had the same vision for the space, for true engagement with the environment; that is what drives his practice.'

The result is this astonishing house, which takes the blurring of inside and outside space to new levels.

A palm tree growing through the middle of the house and emerging triumphantly in a rooftop garden is perhaps the clearest signifier of the extent of the architect's ambition.

'Initially I was worried,' admits Nabili. 'I worried that if we were going to let it out to holidaymakers, would they be comfortable with this level of exposure? In fact, it has worked out better than we could ever have expected and people just love it, none more so than my wife and I.'

How would he summarize the magic of Walatta? 'For me, it's about total calm – the crickets, the frogs, the ocean. It is exactly what I wanted it to be. The very first night I ever spent here was when they had just laid the concrete floor and the roof slab; there were no doors and no windows, nothing apart from the rudimentary skeleton of the structure. I came here and slept on that concrete slab, totally exposed. I always remember the sun rising, and it was heaven. Sometimes I leave doors open, and it still feels just like it did on that very first night.'

A view of Walatta, showing how it blends effortlessly into the landscape, despite the modern and inventive architecture.

The stunning central living space of Walatta unfolds for the visitor. The house is tied together artistically and structurally by cylindrical concrete columns, and the exposed concrete roofs create a raw, industrial energy. However, any hint of brutalism is deftly softened by the 'walls' of natural foliage. The result is one of the most magical rooms in Sri Lanka, recalling, perhaps, the wonder and excitement of a childhood den or a secret garden.

The bedrooms at Walatta continue the jungle theme, and the bare concrete ceilings emphasize the stark bones of this contemporary building, on which so many textures have been artfully laid.

left By its very nature, this house demands a lifestyle exposed to the outside world. However, the discreet sliding doors in the bedrooms facilitate a more enclosed, secure feel at night (and air conditioning for those who wish).

below The stairway at Walatta, with its giant, oversize slab 'steps', reflects the breathtaking scale of the ambition of both owner and architect at this enormously imaginative house.

above A view of the pool from the shady verandah of the house.

left The splendour of Walatta lies in the careful accretion of detail, a classic example of the maxim that with great architecture the whole is much more than the sum of its parts. From the steps descending invitingly into the pool to the elevated rooftop terrace, this house is a fantasy made concrete reality.

KUMARA

There is nothing like an impending party to get a building project moving, and for their 25th wedding anniversary, which fell on New Year's Eve 2009, Australian couple Krissy and Murray McLean had set their hearts on a dramatic dream: forty of their closest friends celebrating with them at their new villa, Kumara, on the southern coast of Sri Lanka. They had bought the land back in 2007, complete with a dilapidated house (which has been completely renovated and is now the staff kitchen), and it is testament to their can-do spirit that they achieved their initial goal. In this light-filled series of pavilions near Mirissa beach, they were able to ring in the New Year with family and friends in true celebratory style. However, building work continued and the couple – who run a scaffolding business in Australia and so are not without experience in the fine art of cajoling builders – only completed the last pavilion in December 2014.

One of the great pleasures of villa living in Sri Lanka is the wonderful staff who attend to your every need at most properties, but at times it can start to feel intrusive. Kumara is cleverly designed to maximize privacy, and a small, semi-sunken kitchen even allows guests to make their own food and drink, should they so desire.

'We do have eight full-time staff at Kumara, but I am very particular about the way I take my coffee,' says Krissy with a chuckle. 'Like lots of people, I like to make it myself. So we really wanted to have a modern kitchen in the main pavilion. It's also very handy for family groups to have a small kitchen there – children like to eat when they are hungry, not necessarily when the food is ready.'

The couple designed the villa themselves with help from a Sri Lankan draughtsman. The main pavilion is decorated with Indian and Sri Lankan artworks and artefacts, and opens out on to a stunning infinity pool, raised several dozen feet above the level of the ground below. It is a perfect place to sit and doze while taking in the sounds of the surrounding jungle.

Such indolence is an activity typically reserved for visitors rather than the owners. 'The only problem is that whenever we do get to Kumara, there is just so much to do that we are always on the go,' says Krissy. 'But now that we have actually finished building, I am looking forward to being able to go there and put my feet up like everybody else.'

Kumara is a wonderfully modern house, but it is also full of antique treasures collected by the owners on their travels around the world. From delicate figurines and religious iconography (far left) to this massive colonial armoire, the modernity of the villa is enriched, enlivened and elevated by the inclusion of surprising and inventive antique pieces.

Kumara is essentially a series of joyful, free-standing pavilions linked not by physical but by mental architecture. The central 'common room' pictured here, complete with a modern kitchen allowing guests autonomy and privacy from the staff, opens on to a delectable poolside area.

top The outside kitchen is populated with the traditional earthenware bowls and cooking implements favoured by many Sri Lankan chefs.

above A daybed on the elevated polished concrete verandah outside a bedroom pavilion makes a perfect location for observing birdlife.

above The stunning pool area is the jewel in the crown that is Kumara. Raised up from the ground, almost at the level of the treetops, this is a special place to soak up Sri Lanka's healing atmosphere. The *ambalama* and the grass growing between the small paving stones create a mellow effect and soften the sharp architectural lines.

CONTEMPORARY

SISINDU T

Charlie Wrey and his wife Tweenie had lived all their married life in a gorgeous 17th-century restored farmhouse in Wiltshire, and had never imagined a day when they would leave England's green and pleasant land. But when the children left home, and a friendly neighbour expressed an interest in buying the place without the involvement of estate agents, they surprised their friends – and themselves – by agreeing to sell up.

As they tried to figure out what to do next, they went to Sri Lanka for a break, visiting a friend near the southern town of Tangalle. Thus began a typically long and winding journey that resulted in the Wreys trading a life of oil bills and crumbling masonry in the English countryside for a paradisical existence in Sisindu T, their self-built tropical fantasy, perched on the top of a model tea estate, with some of the most amazing views in Galle.

These two are clearly great improvisers. 'We blagged our way into running a hotel, which gave us a roof over our heads and time to reflect,' says Charlie of their first few months in Sri Lanka. It was not long before, like so many expats, they somehow found themselves looking at property. When they first saw the site that would become Sisindu T, it was nothing more than jungle – a tea farm with a few grotty outbuildings at the foot of the hill. 'We came up the grassy path lined with pineapples to a summit, with these amazing views, and we both had a dream of building a home here,' recalls Tweenie.

They bought the entire farm – about 8.5 acres (3.5 hectares) – in 2009, and swiftly rebuilt one of the dilapidated sheds as a small bungalow while they set about constructing their dream home on the summit. Their friends back home thought they were 'absolutely potty'; there were moments when they thought they were too. 'There were three months of solid rock blasting before we even laid one foundation,' says Tweenie, but still they managed to build the stunning six-bedroom house in less than two years, start to finish.

The revenues from the tea estate of several acres that surrounds the house help cover costs, giving the couple 'a lovely garden for nothing' as well as providing several local jobs. One of their friends who is 'mad keen on birdwatching' identified no fewer than 141 different species in the garden during a two-week stay.

It should be noted that the Wreys are inveterate hosts, and so a constant stream of friends and family pass through the house. Due to the clever layout of the house, which splits down an east–west axis, revolving around the stunning living area which has a huge tree growing through the middle of it, having guests does not mean having people underfoot. 'It helps that the house is big enough that you hardly see each other,' jokes Tweenie.

121

opposite The central hallway of this stunning house is dominated by a live tree growing up towards the light, mirroring the artificial pillar in remarkable style. Simple furniture made of wood with woven seats and scatter cushions means that rainstorms need not be feared.

above The house is set on a working tea estate, and the jungle is never far from one's thoughts or eye. The oversized earthenware pots were made specially for Charlie Wrey and his wife Tweenie by local craftsmen. The rock paving in the garden was found during excavations in preparation for laying foundations at the house.

above Overlooking the pool and water feature, a bench pushed up against the wall provides the ideal spot for relaxation and reflection. A variety of hats – always a worthwhile accessory to have at hand in the heat – hang overhead with studied insouciance.

opposite A great deal of time is spent in the massive farmhouse-style contemporary kitchen, which would not look out of place in any of London's most desirable suburbs. The chairs were made by local craftsmen, and tropical plants are picked fresh from the garden every day to dress the room.

above, left Colour choices are all-important in Sri Lankan homes, and here the earthy blues work well to provide a sense of coolness throughout the house.

above, centre This compact bathroom offers a homely and tranquil space for the inhabitants of the house or their guests.

above, right Free-standing porcelain bowls add a touch of sophistication in the stylish bathroom.

opposite The main bedroom is dominated by a wooden four-poster bed, made by local craftsmen to a design specified by the owners. The concrete floor is chic and clean, and the atmosphere is notably softened through the use of rugs.

overleaf, above Among the great joys of this house are the outdoor spaces, which cleverly blur the line between inside and outside living. Here, a sitting room is transported to a rooftop, meaning the owners can take in the canopy of the native trees.

overleaf, below Outdoor baths are tremendous fun, especially when, as here, they are raised up to a higher level, giving an unprecedented view from the tub.

page 127 The immaculately detailed swimming pool, laid with small tiles of high-quality stone, shows the importance of choosing the right materials in the outdoor spaces and raises this property to a different level of class. The large loungers in the middle of the photograph are situated on islands within the water, which flows down to the pool.

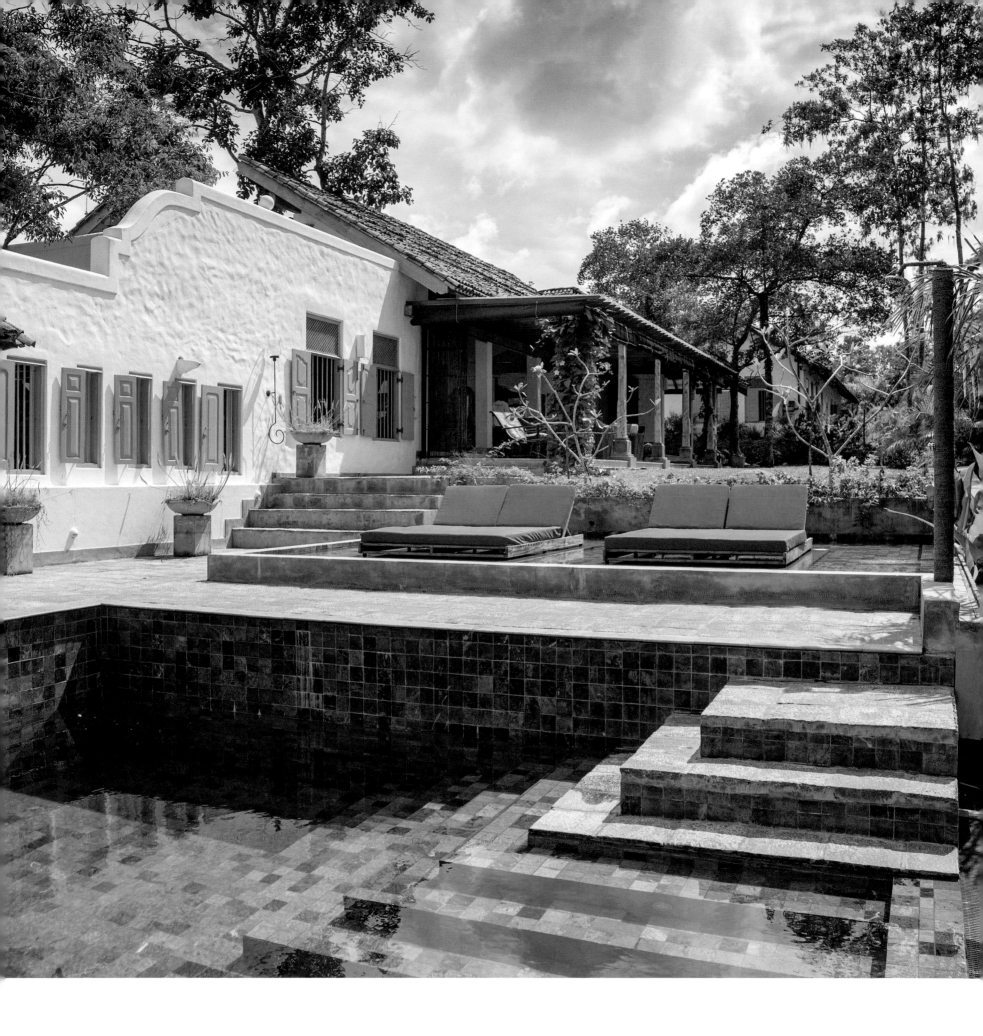

CONTEMPORARY
SATIN DOLL & ELYSIUM

These two houses, both owned by a British–Indian financier and his wife, reflect two sides of the same coin. Satin Doll is a family-friendly, more intimate property, much used by the couple and their young family, while Elysium is a more glamorous, almost palatial villa, ideally suited to entertaining and large gatherings. Both, however, share a vision of laid-back luxury, focused around effortless indoor/outdoor living.

The properties are on nearby plots on the beachfront outside Galle and were designed by the acclaimed Australian architect Bruce Fell-Smith, whose name has become synonymous with a certain cool, contemporary vision of Sri Lankan design. Both properties feature beautifully maintained gardens – home to a family of monkeys and an amazing assortment of birdlife – stretching down to the ocean, where turtles play in the breaking waves. They also house part of the owners' extensive collection of Asian art and antiques.

Satin Doll – named after the Duke Ellington standard by its jazz-loving owner – was formerly an Ayurvedic doctor's house that had been converted into a beach villa by the previous owners. When the present owners acquired the property, it was in a somewhat neglected state. Black paint had been applied to almost every room, and years of sea spray had wreaked havoc on the external appearance of the structure. But Fell-Smith's artful, colonnaded view to the ocean, and the inherent charm and beauty of the property that the couple sensed, was enough to convince them that here was a diamond – rough to be sure, but well worth the effort of polishing, as these pictures show.

Elysium, which Fell-Smith completed in 2005, was in better condition and remains the showstopper. The present owners also undertook extensive renovations and improvements to the property in 2014. It is a more expansive and completely modern property, once again featuring Fell-Smith's distinctive colonnaded aesthetic,

and benefits from the addition of a series of arches leading through to the bedrooms and main living spaces. A magnificent pool leads down to the beach, and there are seating and dining areas inside and outside, under the verandah or the shade of the coconut trees.

Both villas are celebrated locally for the expertise of the staff and the quality of the food from the kitchens. The couple are enthusiastic hosts, and an invitation to lunch at Satin Doll or a party at Elysium is something that you would be crazy to turn down.

Much of the work undertaken in these two houses has been characterized by measured restraint – adding exquisite furnishings while emphasizing the bones of the properties, resisting the temptation to obscure the genius of their creation. Together they make for an interesting and appealing aspect on two complementary takes on Sri Lankan design.

129

above Satin Doll: Australian architect Bruce Fell-Smith designed both houses, which, despite extensive renovations, are unmistakably shot through with his signature vision of contemporary tropical cool.

opposite Elysium's stunning pool area is artfully shaded, making this an ideal spot to relax in the sun.

overleaf, above The stunning sea view from one of the outdoor dining areas at Satin Doll.

overleaf, below The four-poster bed dominates this plain but elegant bedroom at Satin Doll.

right The magnificent central sitting room at Satin Doll evokes the aristocratic glamour of a British stately home, with oversized armchairs and Persian rugs. Note the modern take on traditional Sri Lankan fretwork above the high windows.

top Water features at Elysium convey a sense of tranquillity in the style of grand traditional Sri Lankan homes.

above The trees growing on small islands add a naturalistic touch to Elysium's classic Fell-Smith colonnaded wall.

left Elysium's verandah leads down to a sun platform (overleaf), which looks out over the sea.

CONTEMPORARY

TITTANIYA

Like many other Dubliners working in the property industry, Lisa Forde and Eric Ring of Silk Road Interiors were caught with their metaphorical pants down when the market crashed in 2007. 'We were basically in the business of doing rental fit-outs, designing and making furniture that we were selling through our own store. We mainly sold merchandise from Vietnam, Thailand and Brazil. The crash happened fast, but it took us about six months to clear our decks,' recalls Forde.

Rather than sit at home licking their wounds, the couple decided to head out on the trip of a lifetime. With their 6-year-old son Axel in tow, they spent the next year travelling to thirty different countries, including Turkey, Syria, Jordan, Lebanon and India. Travelling was a cathartic experience, but when they arrived in Sri Lanka, they felt something special: they felt at home. 'We fell in love with Sri Lanka the moment we arrived,' says Forde.

The couple returned home to rent out their house in Dublin and then travelled back to Sri Lanka, buying a small plot of wasteland that was used as a makeshift cricket pitch by the local community. Here, they built a stunning one-storey modernist fantasy, all polished concrete, glass and wood, topped, like a crown, by a roof of shimmering zinc aluminium. They called their villa Tittaniya, after the Sinhalese word for 'playground'. The concrete columns recall the trademark style of the great Geoffrey Bawa, but, as Forde says, 'by putting them on an angle, we are playing with it a bit'.

Importantly, the plot was just yards from Sri Lanka's favourite expat beach, Wijaya, on the southern coast of the island. 'The idea of being in the middle of nowhere is nice, but actually it's kind of important for any Irish person to be in walking distance of the local pub,' chuckles Forde.

The villa was built by the couple themselves, despite having no architectural training. Forde had admittedly worked as an interior designer, but Ring has spent most of his working life as a printer and a rock musician, formerly of Berlin band The Angels. The couple, who now have two children, Axel and Elka, have embraced the opportunity to make a fresh start that living in Sri Lanka has given them. Forde still works in the property industry, fitting out hotels, but Ring has completely reinvented himself as a chef, specializing in Persian and Arabic food.

Life in tropical Sri Lanka is idyllic, although Forde and Ring do miss the 'auld sod'. With the children's education in mind, they plan to take turns living back in Ireland during term time and doing the school run. 'It'll mix it up a bit, to be sure,' says Ring, 'but we have roots in both places now.' Forde expands on this: 'We love Sri Lanka – the people, the weather, the sea, the landscape – but we have realized that the social interaction for the kids is just not enough for us to live here full-time. We are hoping that being home in term time will enable us to have the best of both worlds. It will be another adventure.'

opposite The tranquil courtyard and small pond at the centre of Tittaniya is a modern imagining of Sri Lankan tradition. Smooth polished concrete recalls the work of Bawa, and sliding doors to the bedrooms on either side create a clean, crisp finish.

above A view of the rear of the house, showing the separate bedroom units pictured opposite from another angle. The house is built on former wasteland.

above A circular table draws the eye in the main living space. The custom-made wooden shutters at the end of the room are on rails, enabling them to be 'drawn' like curtains.

right The concrete pillars are a self-conscious nod to the work of Geoffrey Bawa, but by the simple device of turning them on a slight angle, owners Eric Ring and Lisa Forde have created a subtle contemporary twist on the legacy of Sri Lanka's great modern.

above The sitting room emphasizes natural, relaxing tones in the furniture, floor and concrete castings. A picture on the wall, made in part with gold leaf and discovered on the owners' global travels, provides a dazzling flash of colour.

opposite, above Sealed, air-conditioned bedrooms in this contemporary home mean the owners are able to forego the entanglements of mosquito nets, instead allowing the dark teak of the locally made four-poster to dominate. Again, the careful choice of detailing – in this case, bed linen – completes the indulgent feel.

opposite, below These 'jungle bathrooms' are a fantastic illustration of how imaginative owners in Sri Lanka seek to blend luxury with a fantasy of outdoor tropical life. It is hard to imagine anywhere finer to take a morning shower.

CONTEMPORARY
MOUNT CINNAMON

Cinnamon is endemic to Sri Lanka, and the trade in this much-prized spice was one of the reasons why European nations fought so bitterly over the tiny island, with Sri Lanka changing hands between the Dutch, Portuguese and British on many occasions during the colonial era. So when Miles Young, a Hong Kong-based, British-born advertising executive, saw an abandoned cinnamon estate for sale in the hills above Mirissa beach, it immediately appealed to his sense of history. He bought the land, and then, a little later, set about finding an architect to build a home on this remarkable mountaintop.

After speaking to several local architects who failed to impress, Young contacted celebrated Sri Lankan Anjalendran, famous for his authentic, traditional style, whose Crooked House (p. 18) is also featured in this book. 'I was told that he was quite difficult, and he didn't work with foreigners,' says Young, and when a friend of Young's rang Anjalendran for the first time, this impression was certainly borne out. 'Anjalendran told him that he was unavailable to make an appointment as it was Sunday and he was going swimming with his friends, then he hung up on him,' recalls Young.

Eventually a meeting between the two men was organized. However, rather than taking the usual shape of the client interviewing the architect, in this case it was the architect who interviewed the client. After driving around the country with Young for a couple of days, interrogating him on exactly what he thought of various local buildings, Anjalendran was satisfied with his taste, and agreed to inspect the Mirissa Hills site for him, with a view to building a house. The architect drew out the plans for the house, which they named Mount Cinnamon, on a sheet of parchment paper that very day, and the building of the imposing property subsequently diverged very little from that original plan.

What Young and Anjalendran – who have since become firm friends – have achieved together at Mirissa Hills is one of the rare examples of how well Sri Lankans and Europeans can work together when the partnership is an authentic one. The location is quite simply breathtaking, with an extraordinary view over Weligama Bay, which many would argue is the finest coastal view in southern Sri Lanka. The estate has been meticulously restored, with healthy cinnamon trees growing on every patch of the steep-sided land.

Despite being grand, the main house is built very much in the traditional vernacular style favoured by Anjalendran, with a vast pitched roof to protect from tropical heat and rainstorms. The external walls are plastered and 'painted' with local mud. Inside, the central room is divided by a massive sculpture of an 'enchanted forest' created by Sri Lankan artist Laki Senanayake, which has the effect of breaking the large space into two without the interference of a wall. Works of art are a major theme throughout the house.

On the garden level, Young is in the process of creating a good-sized sculpture gallery, with extraordinary pieces hand-picked from local artists. Young and Anjalendran are also building a cinnamon museum a little lower down the hill, where they intend to showcase the machinery and methods, ancient and modern, used in the production of the country's most famous export.

143

opposite The oversize terrace at Mount Cinnamon is pure Anjalendran, based on nothing more complicated than the many *ambalamas* that dot the country.

above Mount Cinnamon is set in breathtaking gardens and, although large, is sensitively designed to complement rather than dominate the landscape.

Antique furniture gives this seating area a warm, casual feel. Anyone seeking to match the wall shade with a paint code can forget about such aspirations: the colour comes from the local mud used to make the traditional plaster.

The colonnaded walkway forms one side of a courtyard surrounding
the pool, leading up to the main living area of the house.

below Mount Cinnamon, as the name suggests, has some of the best views in Sri Lanka, looking out across the plantation to Weligama Bay.

right One of the installations by indigenous artists in the lower ground-floor art gallery. This semi-subterranean space was created by default in the process of levelling the ground floor upstairs and subsequently put to inventive use by the owner.

CLIFFHANGER

The sea is the great passion of the Pringiers family, so little surprise that the remarkable home of Koenraad Pringiers, eldest son of the industrialist Pierre Pringiers and his wife, the artist Saskia Pintelon, is defined by its stunning views of the ocean below. It is a vast, pared-down and futuristic living space. One can easily imagine a cat-stroking Bond villain taking up residence in the clifftop eyrie, keeping a weather eye on troublesome British spies arriving by speedboat on the foaming seas below.

In fact, the Pringiers are among Sri Lanka's most important philanthropists. The family has been a significant employer in Sri Lanka since 1981, when Pierre opened an industrial tyre manufacturer near Weligama Bay. In the early 2000s, Pierre and Koenraad – who works with his father – purchased some land with the idea of building houses near each other, but following the tsunami of 2004, the plans were put on hold as the Pringiers diverted all available resources (and cement) into building 750 houses for local people.

It was not until 2007 that Koenraad felt life for the local community was sufficiently restored to proceed with his own project. He hired the Japanese architect Shigeru Ban, supported by one of Sri Lanka's rising stars, Philip Weeraratne, and finally started work on the two-year project to create Cliffhanger. 'I met Shigeru Ban when he came to Sri Lanka for a tsunami village project in Kirinda, sponsored by family friends,' says Koenraad. 'I asked him to design my house after he had visited the site on the way back from Kirinda to Colombo.' Ban also designed all the furniture in the house, which was produced by Koenraad's brother Jacob, who runs the high-end furniture brand A+ in Colombo.

The house is dominated by the remarkable central living space, its unabashed concrete brutality offset by a woven teak ceiling. The chief function of this space is in giving a panoramic, horizontal view of the ocean, the picture framed by the massive roof, giving the illusion of a cinema screen. In front of this area is the stunning pool, partially covered by a movable deck, which is on rails and can slide across the top of the water. The water feeding the pool also runs constantly around the house in a concrete channel, which not only helps to cool the interior, but also imparts a pleasing feeling of internal logic and vibrancy. The elegant bedrooms, with views of the cliffs, tier off to the sides of the main space, adding volume in the process.

The living space is undoubtedly the showstopper, but there are many other delights to this stunning house, notably the subterranean gym and media room. This downstairs room – a cosy retreat when storms buffet Cliffhanger – is clad in cardboard tubing, a signature of Shigeru Ban, who is famous for his innovative use of paper and cardboard tubing as a construction material (he was the first architect to design and build a house entirely out of paper). A window embedded into the side of the swimming pool adds to the subterranean effect.

Another striking feature is the entrance courtyard, which contains a graceful homage to Bawa – a family friend of the Pringiers – using concrete blocks with triangular perforations. The gardens around the house, based on a cinnamon plantation, are by Sam Soundy, who designed the Butterfly Peace Garden in Batticaloa, on the eastern coast of Sri Lanka. The positioning of the house in the gully of a natural valley ensures that the eye is drawn down the corridor of lush vegetation to the sea beyond.

Cliffhanger is the bold and powerful enactment of a unique architectural imagination, as impressive to behold from a distance as it is up-close. And not a hint of villainy in sight.

Woven wall and ceiling covers and artworks (opposite) soften the brutalist concrete charms of Cliffhanger (above).

The giant dining table in local wood provides plenty of space for the owner to entertain guests. The black-and-white artworks here and elsewhere in the house are by the owner's mother.

above Earthenware pots line the upper and lower levels of this stairway, providing a bridge between old and new aesthetics.

right The wooden shutters allow for the artful play of light and shade in the mezzanine dining area, naturally complementing the muted, calm aesthetic.

above, clockwise from top left The kitchen units are simple but elegant; an antique telescope in the master bedroom peers out over Weligama Bay, evoking pirates and James Bond baddies; a fuller view of the master bedroom; the minimal multilevel bathroom, with solid blinds for privacy.

opposite This outdoor staircase descends over a channel of water, which runs round the entire house, creating a natural cooling effect. The wooden shutters also help to moderate the temperature inside.

The jaw-dropping view of the bay is framed like a projection on a movie screen by the fabric of the villa.

This must surely be one of the most alluring infinity pools in Sri Lanka. For added 'wow', the wooden deck is on rails and can slide to any location in the pool.

LUXURY

Sri Lanka has long been a byword for tropical luxury. Travellers have been drawn to the island in search of peace and indulgence since time immemorial.

What has shifted in recent years is the level of the demand for luxury in Sri Lanka. In the past, it was mainly European expats – especially rich bankers headquartered in Hong Kong – who gravitated towards the Sri Lankan luxury experience, and they were few and far between. Now their numbers are swelling as they are joined by the new Asian tech and industrial billionaires and Russia's super-rich, who are enthusiastically discovering the delights of the country. Wealthy Chinese, many of whom have extensive business and property interests in Sri Lanka,

will be next, observers of the island confidently predict.

The properties featured in this section tend to benefit from enormous budgets. This is often apparent in their scale, but what makes these properties stand out is the emphasis on the living experience. It is the attention to minute details that can make or break a house or hotel – the fittings, the artwork, the colour choices and even the care put into choosing knick-knacks arrayed on the coffee table.

At the forefront of the luxury revolution on the island are the two Aman hotels (pp. 80 & 192). With their extraordinary attention to detail, exacting levels of service and serene spas, these properties have become the standard by which others are

judged. It is notable that several of the most luxurious private houses in Sri Lanka have been created in collaboration with designers and managers who have worked for the Aman group. Also included are two other full-service hotels that are redefining the luxury experience, the Wallawwa and Paradise Road The Villa Bentota.

Top of the list of demands for the super-rich driving this revolution is privacy, not just from other guests, but also from their camera phones – hence the emergence of a new wave of ultra-luxurious private villas within hotels or private villas with hotel levels of service, the very best examples of which are showcased here.

PARADISE ROAD
THE VILLA BENTOTA

Shanth Fernando, the owner of Paradise Road The Villa Bentota, is one of the most important figures in the story of Sri Lankan style. Born to Sinhalese parents in Colombo in 1949, Fernando spent all of his twenties and much of his thirties living overseas, first in the Netherlands and then in Australia before returning to Sri Lanka in 1987, and establishing the highly successful and influential Paradise Road lifestyle stores. His Paradise Road brand is synonymous with a cool, clean and almost exclusively monochrome aesthetic, and Paradise Road The Villa Bentota is the all-encompassing expression of that vision – a private beachside hotel housed in a sensitively renovated Geoffrey Bawa building.

Bawa was originally involved in this unique property in the 1970s, when it was known as the Mohotti Walauwa, and it was Bawa who acquired it and was responsible for converting what was then a dilapidated ancestral home into Sri Lanka's first boutique hotel. For Fernando, who also owns the city's Paradise Road Tintagel Colombo boutique hotel (Prince Charles and the Duchess of Cornwall have stayed there) and one of Colombo's best restaurants, Paradise Road The Gallery Café, the glamorous Villa Bentota is a perfect addition to his portfolio.

'I was born with a talent,' Fernando says. 'To paint. To draw. To appreciate art. My mother saw my talent and fostered it. My father wanted me to be a sportsman or an engineer, so I painted when he was not at home.' Fernando is often accused by critics in Sri Lanka of being an imitator, a charge to which he enthusiastically admits: 'I travel all over the world seeking inspiration. And when something inspires me, I bring the germ of that idea back here and make it my own. I am on a mission.'

After returning to Sri Lanka full-time in 1987, Fernando, a self-confessed 'workaholic', observed that all the leading commercial design in Sri Lanka was 'very colourful and very bright. In Sri Lankan light, bright is not always all that wonderful.' So he started designing his own products, describing the aesthetic he brought to his work as 'essentially black and white'. And that is the way it has stayed. At the Villa Bentota, for example, the beautiful staff sashay back and forth in grey and black sarongs and saris, and the furniture is all upholstered in monochrome stripes.

Without a doubt, the Villa Bentota is an inherently stylish building, with its deco architecture, magnificent pool and indulgent garden stretching towards the sea. Fernando's skill is that his cool adornment makes the property feel both glamorous and tranquil at the same time, creating an easy, natural and relaxed vibe, with rooms and outside areas that make guests feel pampered and special simply by being there. It is easy to lose yourself in the light breeze and the sound of the waves crashing on the beach below.

opposite Each of the private suites at the Villa Bentota enjoys a spacious outdoor seating area, making extensive use of cast concrete furniture softened with textiles, throws and cushions. The impeccably maintained gardens can be glimpsed in the background.

above The oldest part of the property, the original *wallawwa*, was restored and renovated by Geoffrey Bawa. It now forms the reception area of the hotel and backs on to this idyllic pool space, where tea and cake are served every afternoon.

Each of the rooms at the Villa Bentota is unique, and this ground-floor suite makes clever use of light and shade to create a relaxing and private outdoor space. The artwork on the wall expertly complements owner Shanth Fernando's monochrome aesthetic.

left and below The careful use of black and white throughout the Villa Bentota is a key part of the overriding aesthetic of the owner, who believes that monochrome colours work better in the heat of Sri Lanka than the often bright and gaudy shades favoured by some other designers. Note the bed, the base of which is made from a plinth of cast, painted concrete and extends out to form a side table. The pleasing sense of modernity is tempered by the use of traditional furniture and materials.

This small bar area is the perfect place for guests at the hotel to enjoy a pre-dinner drink. The low-key furnishings could be at risk of creating a bland space, but the inventive use of stencilling on the woodwork, which also serves to emphasize the traditional Sri Lankan grilles, elevates this unfussy area into an immersive work of art.

A courtyard-style sitting room in the hotel is given the Bawa
treatment with columns supporting a dark roof, in turn framing,
like a cinema screen, the extraordinary jungle flora. The aim
at the Villa Bentota is to create spaces that are timeless, stylish
and inviting.

above The modernity of the Villa Bentota is cleverly contrasted with antiques and indigenous art.

right This outdoor seating area is an elegant and peaceful space to admire the classic Bawa touches, such as the imposing pillars that frame the view. The carefully tailored table artwork and chandelier fuse timeless grace with style and fashion.

20 MIDDLE STREET

Step inside 20 Middle Street, close the door on the hustle and bustle of the busy streets of Galle Fort, and allow yourself to be struck by the atmosphere of serenity and calm flowing through every detail of this wonderful old property. The shell of the house is believed to date as far back as the 1600s, making it one of the oldest structures in the whole of Sri Lanka, but the property has been skilfully renovated by the dream team of British designer George Cooper and Sri Lanka's very own starchitect, Channa Daswatte. Planning regulations in the Fort are strict, and it took four years to get permission to start work on the house, which had suffered years of neglect.

'When you are working with a historic property, the balance between what to keep and what to update is critical,' explains Cooper. 'The building was ancient but utterly dilapidated, a wreck really. For the physical structure, we simply reinstated what was there, and what had once been there. The house is so remarkable because it incorporates such a range of styles – looking at the columns alone, there were Dutch colonial, English colonial and Portuguese, so the key to the project was finding the right balance.'

Cooper's influence is probably most clearly at work in the sumptuous library, with his signature limewashed and resanded Balinese and Javanese furniture lending an informal yet impressive English note. There are no 'hot' colours; the entire emphasis is on languorous serenity.

What is most striking about the house is the enormity of the space, particularly the cathedral-like, triple-height *zaal*, or sitting room, which is one of the most impressive private rooms in the Fort. 'It is a very grand building,' says Cooper. 'Unlike a lot of houses in the Fort, which are quite low, the height keeps the rooms nice and cool. I was very fortunate because the owners have impeccable taste, and they were very clear in what they wanted: a cool, relaxed environment to enjoy their holidays and perhaps entertain a bit.'

167

With historical references abounding in the architecture of the building, Cooper's achievement is to pull off that toughest of challenges – combining old and new – and simultaneously to create a fresh, contemporary home within the larger historical parameters.

opposite, from top to bottom The genius of this house is in the detail, from the carefully chosen mosquito curtain hooks and traditional umbrellas to these dried and limewashed fruit husks.

above Balinese figurines welcome visitors to the villa.

above The hallway is cool and spacious.

right The delightful verandah area at the front of the house features original stone, carefully restored and relaid. Note also the beautifully restored windows and shutters.

above Pivoting shutters create pleasing geometric regularity in the poolside area.

left The rear verandah is a comfortable outdoor seating area in which friends and family can relax and enjoy everything Sri Lanka has to offer.

above, left George Cooper's signature limewashed and resanded furniture is very much a feature of 20 Middle Street. Balinese artworks are also dotted about the house.

above, right The pale palette lends an aura of tranquillity and peace to every room.

The four-poster in this unfussy
but imposing bedroom was
made to George Cooper's
specifications by local craftsmen
and perfectly complements the
dimensions of the room.

HH

HH, the name given to this luxurious and skilfully finished villa, situated on an idyllic beach just a few miles outside Galle Fort, baffles first-time visitors to Sri Lanka. To insiders, however, the unusual name serves as a convenient shorthand that the gifted interior designer, store owner and hotelier George Cooper – whose KK brand has done so much to advance the cause of Sri Lankan design generally – was closely involved.

In fact, the villa belongs to the same family that owns 20 Middle Street (p. 166), another Cooper-helmed project, although beyond a fondness for the cleansing qualities of whitewashed and resanded timber – a Cooper signature touch – the two properties are as different as chalk and cheese. HH is essentially a series of free-standing pavilions, each perfectly arranged along the extra-wide, sea-fronted plot to give an unobstructed view of the pristine sands and thundering ocean below. The property is, above all, simple, fresh and uncomplicated, designed with nothing more challenging in mind than kicking back and relaxing with family and friends.

HH encapsulates Cooper's universally appealing aesthetic, which is colonial (and post-colonial) tropical and classic British with a modern twist. Terraces add a welcome sense of precision to the overall informal atmosphere.

'I like to under-decorate,' says Cooper. 'I don't like it when you walk into someone's house and it looks like a designer showroom, and you dare not sit down because it is so intimidating. It has got to be comfortable and it has got to be inviting.' He resists the temptation to style individual rooms down to the last detail: 'There has to be room for the owner to have fun, to gather new things – whether that's knick-knacks from their own travels or the odd piece of art or sculpture – and find a place for them in a house. You need things to keep changing and evolving because that's what keeps houses alive. When a house is "finished", it becomes stale.'

HH is a brilliant example of what happens when architecture succeeds in keeping out of nature's way. The pavilions are beautiful, light and airy structures, which impart a feeling of peace, relaxation and well-being. More importantly, however, when the family sits by the pool or under the shade of the towering palms or eats dinner on the terraces, the buildings have a knack of disappearing and making space in the mind and the eye and the soul for the vastness of the ocean.

Beach architecture works best when it tries to do as little as possible. Ironically, creating a successful building that does not seek to assert itself – as opposed to an all-singing, all-dancing pleasure palace – is one of the most demanding challenges that architects and designers can seek to accomplish. Here, there is little doubt of their success.

175

opposite The sun-drenched outdoor seating area by the main pavilion at HH.

above The villa is built right on the sea, on a particularly wide beachfront plot, and the crashing waves of one of the most dramatic coastlines in the region can be viewed from almost any room in the property.

The geometric pattern of the floor engineers a 1920s feel to this fetching beachside boudoir. The furniture is comfortable but practical, as befits a beach villa.

The idyllic poolside area is the perfect place to while away the day.

above This indoor/outdoor seating area and dining room is an elegant reimagining of a traditional *ambalama*.

opposite, above Black-and-white carpeting helps to give a timeless appeal to this charming bedroom, while the bathroom, tucked away behind the bed, is discreet and non-invasive.

opposite, below Luxury villas such as this are increasingly in demand for super-rich and celebrity guests, who require hotel levels of service but want to enjoy their holidays in complete privacy.

THE WALLAWWA

The Sinhalese word *wallawwa* can be roughly translated as 'manor house', and the Wallawwa hotel, located in bucolic countryside just 20 minutes from Sri Lanka's international airport, near Colombo, was once the colonial home of Nicholas Dias-Abeyesinghe, Maha Mudaliyar (Head Chieftain) – a highly prestigious position – under the Dutch in the 18th century. The Wallawwa is a wonderful and impressive example of how, when sensitively and thoughtfully done, the full-scale expansion and renovation of a property from family home to commercial enterprise can become an act of heritage restoration.

Visitors arriving at the hotel are greeted by staff in a deliberately non-corporate 'Welcome Pavilion'. They then follow a winding path along the side of the Pavilion through the immaculate gardens, complete with croquet lawn. At the bottom of the garden, again tucked away behind lush vegetation, is the Wallawwa's shady pool.

Behind the lobby, verandah (on which tea and cake are served in the afternoons) and library lie the Wallawwa's guest rooms and the spa, which revolve around the axis of the central courtyard, where the cooling ponds catch rainwater and house several families of musical frogs. Sofas and daybeds, perfect for dozing off the jet lag and comfortably upholstered in relaxed prints, cool ticking and local batiks, are pushed up casually against the walls. The rooms themselves are luxuriously furnished and dominated by hugely comfortable full-height, artisan-made four-poster beds.

The Wallawwa is a terrific place to start any exploration of Sri Lanka as it provides a living embodiment of so much of the country's history. For example, the original *wallawwa* that stood here is said to have been the most ancient house of its kind in the entire Southern Province. There is good evidence that a building stood on the site as far back as the 18th century. During the Second World War, the property was occupied by the Royal Air Force. In tribute to Lord Mountbatten, who was Supreme Allied Commander of the strategically important South East Asia Command during the latter years of the Second World War, a small two-bedroom self-contained apartment has been created within the hotel. With its own private pool and room service, it is a place where celebrities and other high-profile guests can enjoy total privacy.

It is this history, and the Wallawwa's tranquil surroundings, that transport anyone arriving through the gates back in time and away from the speed and stress of the outside world. The Wallawwa is also celebrated in Sri Lankan circles for the excellence of its kitchens, with fruit and vegetables coming from the hotel's own 5-acre (2-hectare) garden, which opened in 2013, and through which guests are welcome to take a tour.

opposite, above This inviting walkway, decorated with the hotel's signature blue stripes and cleverly softened with tropical planting, leads visitors to and from the guest rooms.

opposite, below (left to right) Carrom boards can be found throughout the hotel to entertain guests; the signature stripes bring a sense of calm to the spa area; an earthenware pot emphasizes the natural, organic philosophy behind the hotel; a verandah and seating area, perfect for enjoying afternoon tea.

above The immaculate gardens at the Wallawwa recall an English country idyll.

The hotel devotes great energy to creating enticing outdoor spaces. These cast concrete sofa and chair bases, with loose cushions for comfort, withstand the extreme rigours of the Sri Lankan climate.

right The relaxed nature of the Wallawwa helps inculcate a local feel to what is undoubtedly one of the most extraordinary airport hotels in the world.

below The colonial heritage of the building is amply demonstrated by these pillars, supporting the massive overhang of the roof in the main building. The pillars along the outer edge are based on traditional Dutch colonial architecture. The classic wicker chairs complete the look.

left Much of the food served to guests comes from the organic farm attached to the garden. Bananas, pineapples, peppers and salad leaves are all grown here in abundance throughout the year, and fresh flowers to decorate rooms and public areas are also plucked from the farm every day.

opposite The pool is tucked away in jungle, making it particularly seductive and refreshing. The use of high-quality stone in the pool adds a distinguished touch. The stripe theme of the hotel is continued with the cushions on the wicker pool loungers, with the shelter in the corner providing respite on sweltering days.

INDISCH

Indisch, a sumptuous Raj-style villa located in the small town of Ahangama, 12 miles (20 km) south of Galle, is one of the most indulgent holiday houses Sri Lanka has to offer. The substantial house, owned by Australian businessman David Dawborn and his wife Elizabeth, is arranged around a small central courtyard, which perfectly frames a koi carp pond and fountain. The house has five superbly appointed bedrooms and a vast, sweeping staircase that recalls a British stately home. The interior is decorated with the Dawborns' extensive collection of colonial-era antiques, Buddhist statues and modern art from around Asia.

The exterior of the building is dominated by an oversized verandah, perfect for taking afternoon tea and cake as the sunlight glitters off the deliciously large T-shaped pool, which juts out towards one of the most picturesque beaches for miles around. This is the star attraction of the immaculately maintained garden, which, unusually among houses in Sri Lanka, also boasts a Jungle Gym climbing frame for kids. A humble gate leads from the garden to the beach, where you can walk on the soft sand and admire the sight of Sri Lanka's famous stilt fishermen, balancing on poles driven into the sand a few dozen yards out at sea, from which they drop their rods into the water.

The food at Indisch is a particular highlight. Much of the produce used in the kitchen is grown organically at a small farm owned by the house, a marked trend among luxury establishments in the country as increasingly demanding guests seek greater assurances over the provenance of their food. Many guests – despite the cohort of sixteen staff – are tempted back into the kitchen by the prospect of lessons with the masterful chef, one of Sri Lanka's finest, who will happily teach holidaymakers how to make his signature curries. Lessons (over traditional wood fires) can even be carried out in the free-standing curry house in the garden.

David bought the land on which Indisch stands after a 40th birthday holiday in Sri Lanka 'got out of control'. 'We have lived in Indonesia for twenty-five years now, and we had always dreamed about somewhere like Sri Lanka for our retirement,' says David. 'But we have four children, and one of the drivers was a place for family to have holidays, hence the play equipment. Although we looked at a lot of other places, the land on which Indisch is built is actually one of the first places we were shown.'

The American architect Richard Emory, who has worked extensively with the Aman group, was heavily involved in the planning and design of the house between 2005 and 2006. The villa was not completed until 2012.

'We had a particular vision of barefoot luxury in mind,' says David. 'Big rooms, high ceilings, great art and classic, antique furniture. It took us a few years to get it together, but I think we got there in the end.' Few would disagree with that assessment.

187

opposite, left The magnificent pool stretches out towards the ocean, occupying a unique headland, making this an enviable location on the coast.

opposite, right The owners' extensive art collection, gathered on travels around the tropical world, lends a sense of gravity and antiquity to the otherwise new building.

above The bedroom balconies on the first floor offer unrivalled views of the sea.

above With a massive house such as this, airflow is provided by the central courtyard, seen here with an antique pot in the foreground.

left This villa is all about indulgent living. The magnificent T-shaped pool dominates the garden, which is meticulously maintained by an army of staff. The palm trees testify to the former use of the land as a plantation in the British colonial era.

An expert blend of old and new, the bedrooms at Indisch are furnished with select antique pieces.

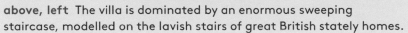

above, left The villa is dominated by an enormous sweeping staircase, modelled on the lavish stairs of great British stately homes.

above, right The owners are avid art collectors and the villa provides a wonderful opportunity for them to display the remarkable items brought back from their travels around the world.

LUXURY

AMANWELLA

Peace is the watchword of the Aman hotels, and peace is what you will surely find at Amanwella, located on a stunning crescent-shaped beach on the southern coast of Sri Lanka. Indeed, the name Amanwella is derived from the Sanskrit for 'peace' (*aman*) and the Sinhalese word for 'beach' (*wella*).

The resort offers twenty-seven suites, each boasting its own private plunge pool and terrazzo terrace. As any Aman 'regular' would expect, the suites are in the hotel group's classic style, characterized by a minimalist aesthetic, but are designed to be culturally appropriate and complement the resort's natural setting as far as possible. The terrazzo floors are finished in muted sandy tones to reflect the beach setting, and indigenous building materials and techniques are used as much as possible. Examples include the distinctive terracotta roof tiles and hand-hewn stone walls, and the furniture is also made largely from local kithul wood.

Like all the best Sri Lankan rooms, the suites open on both sides to let in cooling sea breezes, but for lovers of air conditioning, the floor-to-ceiling glass and latticed panels can be eased into place and the cold air allowed to flow. The rooms are cleverly laid out with large timber sliding panels, which separate the interior space into a combined sleeping/living room and an open-plan bathroom. The sleeping/living room features a luxurious king-size bed into which guests can collapse after a hard day of lounging in the sun, as well as a writing desk, an armchair and a daybed.

There are typically four members of staff to every guest. As at all Aman resorts, there is no reception desk, lobby or bellboy, giving the illusion of staying at a private house – an illusion that can be pleasantly shattered at any moment simply by picking up the phone and ordering room service. Rambling pathways connect the suites to the library, the Bawa-inspired lounge, the yoga platform on the beach and the oceanside restaurant.

One particularly striking aspect of Amanwella is the large red courtyard that leads visitors to the arrival pavilion. Inspired by Sri Lanka's most notable modern architect, Geoffrey Bawa, the arrival pavilion is a breezy, colonnaded, open-air structure overlooking a grassed courtyard and a reflection pool.

Also hard to overlook is the 155-ft (47-m) infinity pool, with jaw-dropping vistas of the coconut grove, the beach and the sea beyond. Views from the ample terraces are of the ocean and the beach, which is flanked by two magnificent rocky headlands. Peace? Most certainly.

opposite The walkways linking the luxurious separate rooms at Amanwella are of a carefully textured, honey-coloured stone.

above Lily pads float serenely in one of the many ponds that dot the hotel, which has become a byword for peaceful sophistication.

above Private outdoor seating areas connected to each room are furnished with clean, modern pieces. The cast concrete grille, painted white, is a clear tribute to Bawa.

right The library at Amanwella, an air-conditioned temple of peace, is the ideal spot to shelter from the midday heat.

overleaf The light and airy breakfast room.

above Another tribute to the geometric genius of Geoffrey Bawa is to be found in this piece of sculpture, which greets guests as they arrive at the hotel.

left The infinity pool gives on to a serene view of the ocean.

VISITING SRI LANKA

Visitors to Sri Lanka can apply for a thirty-day visa online. This can be extended to ninety days at the Department of Immigration & Emigration in Colombo.

It is often claimed that Sri Lanka has more public holidays than any other country in the world. On these days, little business can be accomplished. The exact dates can be found online, but a good starting point is to remember that every full moon is a *poya* day and all government offices, big shops and banks are closed.

It is also worth noting that in Sri Lanka the head gestures for 'yes' and 'no' are reversed, with nodding indicating disagreement, which can lead to confusion and misunderstanding among tourists.

Many of the villas featured in this book can be rented for private stays. Most villas have their own websites, which can be found online. Some of the villas are managed by Jack Eden and can be booked through Villas in Sri Lanka (villasinsrilanka.com).

For excursions, adventures and itineraries, Experience Travel Group (experiencetravelgroup.com) is a good place to start. Manjula Kumara provided us with a reliable and comfortable car service (+94 77 362 8685 or manjula_kumara@hotmail.com).

ACKNOWLEDGMENTS

A book such as this cannot be accomplished without help from innumerable sources. James and I were lucky to be assisted every step of the way, and we would particularly like to thank all the owners who made their homes available to us.

Thanks to Jack and Jo Eden of Eden Villas and to Hen Tatham of Kikili House (kikilihouse.com) for persuading so many of the owners to open their doors to us.

A big thank you to Sam and 'Mudhouse Tom' at the Experience Travel Group for help, inspiration and transport around Sri Lanka.

Thank you also to Meg and Phil at Sri Lanka's best poster shop, Stick No Bills (sticknobillsonline.com), for political and cultural insight. The reproduction and vintage Sri Lankan posters seen in some pictures can be bought at the Stick No Bills shop in Galle Fort or online.

Thanks to Shanth Fernando. Many villa owners in Sri Lanka furnish their houses with work from the designer's Paradise Road stores (paradiseroad.lk).

And last but not least, thanks to Geoffrey Dobbs for his hospitality and encouragement.

FURTHER READING

Anil's Ghost, Michael Ondaatje, London: Vintage Books, 2011

Anjalendran: Architect Of Sri Lanka, David Robson, photographs by Waruna Gomis, North Clarendon (VT): Tuttle Publishing, 2009

The Architectural Heritage of Sri Lanka: Measured Drawings from the Anjalendran Studio, David Robson, photographs by Dominic Sansoni, London: Laurence King, 2015

Bawa: The Sri Lanka Gardens, David Robson, photographs by Dominic Sansoni, London: Thames & Hudson, 2009

Beyond Bawa: Modern Masterworks of Monsoon Asia, David Robson, photographs by Richard Powers, London: Thames & Hudson, 2014

Cinnamon Gardens, Shyam Selvadurai, London: Anchor, 1999

The Fountains of Paradise, Arthur C. Clarke, London: Gollancz, 2001

Geoffrey Bawa: The Complete Works, Geoffrey Bawa and David Robson, London: Thames & Hudson, 2002

An Historical Relation of the Island Ceylon, Robert Knox, London: Richard Chiswell, 1681

Living in Sri Lanka, James Fennell & Turtle Bunbury, London: Thames & Hudson, 2006

Living Modern Tropical: A Sourcebook of Stylish Interiors, Richard Powers, text by Phyllis Richardson, London: Thames & Hudson, 2012

Lunuganga, Geoffrey Bawa, photographs by Christoph Bon and Dominic Sansoni, Singapore: Times Editions, 1990

Sri Lanka Style: Tropical Design and Architecture, Channa Daswatte, photographs by Dominic Sansoni, Singapore: Periplus Editions, 2006

Ultimate Tropical, Luca Invernizzi Tettoni, London: Thames & Hudson, 2008

INDEX